MW01166586

The Success Effect. Copyright © 2005 by John Eckberg . All rights reserved. Copyright under the Berne Copyright Convention, Universal Copyright Convention and Pan-American Copyright Convention.

No part of this book may be used or reproduced, stored in a retrieval system or transmitted in any form, or by any means, electronic, mechanical, photocopied, recorded or otherwise, without written permission of the publisher except in the case of brief quotations embodied in critical articles and reviews.

Published by Sterling & Ross Publishers
New York, NY 10001
www.SterlingandRoss.com

Cover design by Brian Goff
Composition/typography by Polina Bartashnik

Library of Congress Cataloging-in-Publication Data
Eckberg, John, 1953-
  The success effect : uncommon conversations with America's business trailblazers / by John Eckberg.
     p. cm.
  ISBN 0-9766372-4-3
  1. Success in business--United States. 2. Businesspeople--United States--Interviews. I. Title.

HF5386.E218 2005
658.4'09--dc22

2005023462

10 9 8 7 6 5 4 3 2

Printed in the United States of America.

Keith,
Enjoy your time with those girls!
John Eckberg

THE SUCCESS EFFECT:

Uncommon Conversations with America's Business Trailblazers

By John Eckberg

S&R
PUBLISHERS

NEW YORK   TORONTO   LONDON

For Carol

Contents

· ·

AUTHOR INTRODUCTION

"But at my back I always hear, Time's winged chariot hurrying near, And yonder all before us lie, Deserts of vast eternity."

—Andrew Marvel

I remember standing at the workbench back behind the furnace in the basement with my father, Stanley, as he soldered tiny red and orange-striped cylinders onto a circuit board. They were resisters, my father told me, electronics about the size of a pencil eraser, and the color of the stripe was a clue to that particular resister's ability to manipulate the flow of electrons.

His words meant nothing to me. What I knew was that my father was building a HAM radio and would be able to listen and eventually talk to people from all over the world in International Code. I was young, in second grade, and didn't understand the meaning of HAM radio, but I liked the name because I liked ham. What I could gather was that my father was feeling the pull of a greater world from down there in our basement, and he was doing something few other fathers could do. He was building a radio. He'd been making radios of one kind or another since he was a boy back in the 1920s.

The parts to this one were beyond appealing: panels of stainless steel for the outside skin and within, a chassis holding copper coils, sub-layers of resisters and capacitors with a few glass tubes lording over the whole assembly. And while it took him months to build, when it finally came to life, the receiver yowled and keened from an open speaker on the workbench, signaling that the radio receiver was honing in on a transmission, perhaps another operator in their basement; somebody from Australia, South Africa or Europe. The outside world came floating into that gray basement on the edge of a cornfield south of Akron, Ohio, in a strange and tweaky symphony of static, beeps and binks.

His transmitter came to life on the day he strung his homemade antenna: 100 yards of heavy wire that reached from the roof of our house to the upper limbs of a distant cherry tree. I remember a giant of a guy, at six-foot-six, way up in the crown of the tree where only an adventurous boy would ever dare to climb. The tree swayed dangerously in the wind, yet there was my father, clinging to the trunk with one arm and pulling the heavy wire with the other.

That afternoon he connected his homemade bronze telegraph key, and in a flurry of blinks and beeps, he began to talk to people from the other side of the world. I thought of my late father while interviewing Dave Pelz, the Texas golf swami to pros and hackers alike. Pelz is, after all, a rocket scientist. He worked on the nation's space program from the floor of Mission Control. My father, too, was a rocket scientist but worked on the floor of a Subroc missile factory, building anti-submarine missiles for the Armed Services.

I always tell people some of my father's story when they ask about my hometown or my background. After all, how many people had a father who was a rocket scientist? So I told Pelz, too. "They don't make men like him anymore," I said.

On the other end of the phone line, Pelz was silent. He must have realized that it just wasn't true, that men like my father were being born everywhere in America all the time, and they always would be around; curious and driven, dreamers and doers, and intelligent beyond what was, in my late father's case, an eighth grade education.

Of course, Pelz was too polite to suggest otherwise. The ingenuity and ambition of average and not-so-average Americans has always been a marvelous thing to behold, and it is far more common than most people realize. Nobody knows this better than Pelz, who has turned his back on space exploration to create a golf instruction dynasty of traveling and resort-based instructors that generates millions of dollars in annual revenues.

Pelz was on a short but growing list of remarkable or interesting people I had interviewed as a business reporter at *The Cincinnati Enquirer*. The list was as varied as the supply-and-demand waves of commerce that many Americans surf to wealth and prominence.

I sometimes forget what a beautiful thing it is to be a

reporter at a big city newspaper. How many people get to ask questions of others for a living, and then get paid to ponder, analyze, and report on the thoughts and insights within their answers?

It is an immense, daily privilege and honor to work on a newspaper. And it is almost always fun, hardly work at all, not like, say, putting asphalt roofs on buildings on steamy summer days or working in a dingy factory. It's a job, of course, but it's more like being paid to be a lifelong, curious five year-old.

My style as a business reporter is to ask people questions about issues that appeal to me, and hope that the answers will resonate with readers. Sometimes, after working up a story from a particularly interesting interview, I would save the tape and drop it into my desk drawer. One day I looked into that drawer and realized that a "few" tapes had grown into a sizeable collection, and that perhaps there were insights on those tapes that I had missed, or by necessity had edited out when writing my stories.

I wondered, was there a book in my desk drawer? Perhaps. But like newspaper stories, a book's essential material is too often filtered through the eyes of the writer. Why not, instead, create a book of insight and experience direct from the tapes; the pure and unadulterated thoughts of the executives and other personalities. I soon found that, indeed, the stories told by these men and women did offer a road map to success. Some had real estate empires at their command, moguls like Donald J. Trump and Sam Zell. Some employed workers by the thousands like Dan DiMicco of Nucor. Or, like Peter Block, they advised companies from all over the world on the best approaches to gain a worker's devotion, respect and labor.

Others offered suggestions on how workers could better realize happiness and fulfillment on the job, how managers could diffuse difficult people, or even how to prepare for an upcoming presentation or speech.

These strategies on business practices were as varied as a beam of light through a prism. IDEO's Tom Kelley told companies to seek insight everywhere but mostly in the aisles of big box retail stores or local grocery stores. Some, like Dr. Karen Stephenson, charted career paths that mixed bravado with brains. She had spent a good part of her life chasing zephyrs, seeking wisps of anthropology in the rain forests of South America and a dozen other distant places around the globe for insights that would yield wisdom about hidden networks of influence that pervade each and every culture, each and every company.

True stories are always more compelling than fiction, and so too, I found, with these conversations about the corners of American commerce. Here, stories, themes, and approaches to business, as well as to life, emerged and they had impact and resonance. The incredible saga of the late Ohio businessman Dave Longaberger, is a perfect example, particularly when told through the eyes of his daughter, Tami.

Longaberger was a frugal bread truck driver and family man who saved his dimes to buy a little restaurant and a few years later a small town grocery store. When Dave saw how people were drawn to his father's handmade baskets, he took out yet another loan, risking everything in the process, to create a basket company that within a few decades heaved billions of dollars to the top line of the balance sheet while creating tens of thousands of jobs, and wealth for the Longabergers beyond belief. Giant oak trees do indeed grow from tiny acorns and sometimes so do big businesses.

An unquenchable curiosity fueled other innovators. Robert Robinson Sr. was puzzled by the crude, rag-on-a-stick approach to the sordid business of cleaning bathrooms, which had prevailed as the toilet-cleaning system of choice in the western world for century upon century. One day, the mechanical engineer in Robinson came to life and he developed a new machine and a new way to clean restrooms. His story and dozens of others emerged from that desk drawer in the teller's own words.

Dean Butler's tale shows what can happen when serendipity meets initiative, when ambition flows in harmony with will. Many entrepreneurs share this trait: they are able to envision and embrace an idea, then get others moving in the same direction.

"Successful performance in any effort begins with the expression of an idea," says performance expert Doug Newburg.

Newburg's specialty is dissecting the incredible will to win that pervades benchwarmer and stellar athlete alike. He concludes that the schmoes and the pros come from the same space: both have a drive, but some are luckier or work harder, others are just wired better than anybody else. "What can be perceived as a relaxed lack of effort is merely the absence of tension," he says, "because peak performance is never an effortless endeavor."

The trick is to get others in an organization to model Newburg's approach. Golf swami Pelz also believes that most people are capable of peak achievement at any time and says the best golf game for everybody should be the next round played.

These interviews are slices of time, and snapshots of success. Some interviewees focus on the power of mission. Others say it is will that transforms reality. Insights from the interviews are sometimes too fleeting, the provocative thinking is sometimes brief. Many of the questions posed in this book simply give rise to other questions. For example, why would Donald J. Trump's father saddle him with a miserable apartment complex in Cincinnati, Ohio—a dog of a project, one that was virtually empty? Did he want to offer his son a genuine challenge so the newly minted graduate could sip the nectar of true success? Or was too much at stake in one Midwestern real estate wager for a family fortune already stretched thin? Trump had to live in Cincinnati for nearly a year and that, alone, says much. Young bon vivants do not willingly give up the glitz of Manhattan or the patina of South Beach to move to a place like Cincinnati. Trump, apparently, had a job to do.

Interview topics sprawl across a broad band of issues. Deepak Chopra created a group to explore transformations of individuals and organizations, while Gladys Gossett Hankins believes she can change a racist's heart. Bengal Coach Marvin Lewis talks about the steps needed to turn losing teams into winners.

When seeking parallels between business innovators, another trend becomes clear: the greatest head start of all in our society is capital and access to it. The best idea withers without it.

What did E.W. Scripps' board members say and think in

private when tens of millions in losses mounted year after year from the birth of HGTV and the Food Network? Where was this so-called cable revolution, the new radio? Would this start-up division ever begin to turn a profit and justify the pricy satellite and all-digital library in Knoxville?

When the revenue reversal finally arrived, profits took off like a rocket, and the flow of cash made the media company a darling of Wall Street. It came at a time when the rest of the economy and most media companies were mired in recession. How did it happen? Who was in charge? Where was the inspiration?

The executive behind the idea of a cable network dedicated to houses, gardens, kitchens, and food was a TV Vice President within the Scripps organization—Kenneth S. Lowe. His notion of a network carrying advertising and content concerning the stuff of everyday life—and not just another network of lame sitcoms—was pure genius. How could others have missed this opportunity? Lowe knew it was not far-fetched. The day he presented his concept to the board of directors, he had a magazine rack full of publications as evidence of the size of the ad market they would go after. When the network launched, the phones to the Knoxville studio were jammed.

Or is the generation of wealth merely a manifestation of the old saying: the rich will always get richer? Wealth creates more wealth? After all, few fathers even have one apartment to give to a son to manage and then sell, let alone 1,164. So silver and gold go to those who already have it; business and commerce devolve, ultimately, into the simple notion that those born into the lucky sperm and ovary club of wealth will always win? But if that's true, how then to explain the life of real estate mogul Sam Zell, who started out in a 10-by-12 foot office and now controls a handful of companies, including one that owns 123 million square feet of class A office space? "Do not make small plans," Zell advises.

And what to make of Jerry Springer? He was an activist and campus organizer for Bobby Kennedy who decided to run for a local office in Cincinnati, Ohio, in the 1970s. Although he was a lawyer, Springer hated law and soon did not have much use for a local elective office, either. A failed run for governor led to a new career as local TV news anchorman and, finally, to that of ribald talk show host. Careers can't really be planned, he says. And ambition isn't something from a can.

There are many such stories here, tales of people who envisioned a future, a career, or a product, and watched it happen or made it happen through personal effort and force of will. As one HAM radio operator learned five decades ago from the basement of a small house on the edge of a farmer's field outside of Akron, words from afar can transform worlds, change lives, and create happiness. May you get some sense of this power in the following conversations.

John Eckberg

1

✸Good Habits

David Pelz, *Golf Coach to PGA Greats*

Dave Pelz was a NASA physicist who turned his back on space research to create a golf coaching niche that first transformed—then grew the industry of golf instruction.

Pelz believes the game creates bonds for all who play because of the social nature of the sport and the competition inherent in any game. Pelz knows a little about battles of will on a golf course. As a Big 10 college golfer with a four-year golf scholarship to Indiana University, he found that he simply couldn't beat another Big 10 player, Jack Nicklaus. After twenty-two attempts to beat him (and not knowing Nicklaus was the best in the world), Pelz turned away from a hoped-for spot on the PGA tour and instead focused his career on the physics of space and satellite development.

Competition and the recreation provided by golf have transformative powers, Pelz insists. It can change lives and even the direction of companies as many executives have found out. From teaching short game skills, where Pelz found 80 percent of lost strokes occur, to developing training aids based on his physics research, Pelz has newcomers, executives and top pros beating a path to his door.

Question: Golf and space—tell me about Alan Shepherd.

Answer: Alan Shepherd was the golfing astronaut, really a golf nut. He took the clubs up there and hit balls on the moon.

Q: That's pretty impressive right there. You've been interviewed—oh, probably a couple of thousand times—so here's a question I hope you haven't heard: do salesmen who are lousy golfers get more clients than salesmen who are great golfers?

A: Hah, heh! I think the better players who still manage to lose without being noticeable do the best. Losing like this is an art. Everybody respects the good game, especially the client who is really trying to play well. He respects the player who can play well. But he loves to beat that guy, too. When a putt just lips out or an iron shot hits on the edge of a bunker and then rolls down in, this guy gets and deserves the client's respect. He has managed to let the client win without being detected. The salesman who does this will be successful, as well as the ultimate manipulator on the golf course.

Q: How did golf become this 7,000-yard long office? Has it always had that patina in America?

A: I think that originally, when only the wealthy played, it was because the wealthy would go out and they would have tremendous seclusion and privacy. It's such a great venue. You don't have to be great to play. Even if you play poorly, you can enjoy it out there. So it becomes a pleasant experience for both players. And the pace is relaxed. Between shots you have a lot of time to talk. You bond with each other, fighting the game together, trying to score well, and yet there is this element of relaxed time in a natural setting. That's as good as or maybe better than sitting in a plush office or restaurant looking out at a beautiful view with nice ambiance, comfortable chairs, good food and good wine.

There are a number of corporations that buy schools and clinics from us. In a three-day school, we normally have 16 people. But sometimes a company will buy it and bring six or eight key clients with one or two of their own employees from the sales or marketing group. The bonding experience that these eight or 10 people have together, learning the game together for 70 percent of every day is terrific. They're totally focused and completely consumed by learning to play the game better. Then the other 30 percent becomes an unbelievable bonding experience with camaraderie, togetherness and the fun you have and difficult times and frustrations you share. So it is, in fact, a wonderful place to do business.

We have a number of companies that do this because it is not perceived as a sales experience when you're all together trying to learn to play the game.

• •
CDs in the Changer

"'A Better Place to Be' by Harry Chapin may be my favorite song of all time."

Country Roads: Greatest Hits of John Denver by John Denver

The Very Best of Willie by Willie Nelson

Killin' Time by Clint Black

• •

Q: Many, many women have entered the workforce in the past 30 years, but much golf still remains to be played by them. They feel excluded. To break in, you have that age-old barrier—it's a difficult game. It's a challenge even for the best golfers. Are golf lessons an investment with payback—personal and professional?

A: Oh, absolutely! There is absolutely no question

of that. Men are very impressed with the way women play golf, if they play at all well. Now, I don't mean that the new, executive businesswoman has to be a great player, but she has to know about the game, respect the game and be able to play quickly enough. It's not what she scored, it's how well she addresses the ball, and how well she moves on the course. Nobody wants to stand around and wait for you. Nobody else wants to worry about your problems. Men and women who are self-conscious about the way they play are totally misguided. It's not what you score. It's how well you play the game and move around the course. Handicaps adjust for the skill levels. But if you can play to your handicap in a reasonable amount of time and not throw clubs and complain about your bad shots, then you can be an enjoyable playing partner. That's the wonderful thing about golf. If you can get past worrying about your own game, then you are in great shape because you can really have fun with other people.

Q: Are you seeing more women in your classes?

A: Oh, when we started our schools, it was almost 10 percent women and that was in 1987. Last year, there were 25 percent, and it just grows every year. We not only have husbands that bring their wives but we have a lot of wives who bring their husbands. We have a number of families where the golfer of the family is the wife, and she drags the husband in.

Q: Golf offers the possibility of huge public embarrassments...

A: It does, but any golfer knows that. I played the other day with a good friend who is on the PGA tour, and he hit some bad shots that he was not particularly proud of, but he hadn't been playing much and dealing with rehabbing an injury, but golf is a very humbling game. But I don't make fun of him and he doesn't make fun of me when I hit a bad shot.

We understand the game is tough. Everybody who plays it a lot and anybody who plays it seriously will hit bad shots. You have to get over that. It's part of the game.

It's a humbling game. And if you think you're going to go out and intimidate the game or never be embarrassed, then take up another sport. Don't take up golf. It's one of the wonderful things about it and that's why it's such a bonding experience.

The game is bigger than any of us. It's bigger than Nicklaus. It's bigger than Palmer. It's bigger than Norman. It's bigger than Woods. It's bigger than any of us, and it's bigger than all of us combined. It has been—and it will remain—a great game for centuries to come, and that's what makes it such a wonderful place to bond with people.

• •

BOOKS ON THE NIGHTSTAND

"I very seldom read. I've never read a golf book, although I have read parts of 'Golf in the Kingdom'."

• •

Q: I think that lives have pivot points. What was the pivot point for you when you just finally said, "I've got to walk away from science and go back to this sport that has a grip on me?"

A: I'd always been a golfer. I went to school so I could learn to play well enough to go on the [PGA] tour and become a pro. That was my goal. I didn't major in physics so that I could go to Goddard's Space Flight Center and do space research; I went to Indiana University for four years to learn to play golf. As I look back now, I did the practice reps but I did the wrong reps.

In hindsight, I saw that it was the classic example of practicing the wrong thing, practicing the wrong way and getting worse rather than better. 40,000 reps of the wrong thing will do that! I have since learned that when you practice something the wrong way, all you do is groove the wrong thing. If you're a poor practicer, you will become permanently poor at whatever you are attempting to do. All I did was groove all my bad habits.

So I gave up golf and got a great job at Goddard Space Flight Center in Greenbelt, Maryland, doing space research because I had the physics education. For 15 years I did space research and did golf as a hobby. I have seen men walk on the moon. I have been standing there at Mission Control [before Houston was built, Goddard was the Control Center for the entire space effort] seen the men walk on the moon, loving my work, loving every day of work. But I'm looking at who else is in the world of physics and what they're doing, and a startling thing occurred to me.

I realized that if I worked all day in physics, every day for the rest of my life, I would not be the best physicist. I would not be the best research scientist because so many people were smarter than I was. I thought that if, on the other hand, I really worked hard at golf—I had learned a lot, I had done some research projects at that time and I had already learned why I was never a great player—I thought maybe if I take my physics education, if I take my experience as an experimentalist as a research scientist at Goddard doing space research, and if I took it all into golf, maybe I could be the best help to golfers that there's ever been.

Even though I was sitting in the control center at Goddard and watching guys walk on the moon, I was thinking about golf. I was thinking why I shot 69 the week before when I could have had a 67 or 66. That's who I am. I love to do research in golf. That's my first love. It's golf. It's not space, even though I love space. What makes golf so great to me is that you can learn it. I have a goal that at age 70, I will be the best player I have ever been. I'm not saying I'll be the best player who's ever lived. All I want to be is the best I've ever been.

Q: Forty thousand reps and the same stroke, it has to be the dullest thing on earth…

A: No, no, no. It's really quite exciting actually. The background of my effort to be a great player, you have to understand, is that as a physics major, it's not real easy. I went to the golf course everyday, rain or shine—24/7. I was focused on golf my senior year and I was going to be the best golfer in the Big 10. I was going to win the NCAA tournament. That was my goal. So who wins the Big 10? Jack Nicklaus. Who wins the NCAA? Jack Nicklaus. Who wins the matches on my home course? Jack Nicklaus. He was a better golfer.

Q: But he was a better golfer than anybody on earth. You didn't see it that way?

A: We didn't know that. Heavens, no. He was a fat kid. And this was Big 10 golf and we called him names and he was beating us like a drum. We didn't realize how good he was but I had to think that I had to do something special because I'd been beaten by him my freshman, sophomore, and junior seasons. And it just continued and I wanted to win.

So, I went to the golf course. I only had nine hours of courses. I was done with school every day at 11 a.m. and I was at the golf course, hitting balls or playing seven days a week at noon—'til dark. I said, "I'm going to do it," and after having put that effort forth, I couldn't make it. I didn't have the instruction that I needed to learn how to be a better player so all I did was learn how to become a more consistently mediocre player.

And that is part of what has driven me. Once I realized that and started making measurements in the game, and found out what I was really weak in and created feedback devices to give me feedback on what I was really weak in, I started getting better and became a much better player.

I was far better after college as a space research scientist at Goddard Space Flight Center in Maryland. I became the best player I'd ever been simply because I started practicing and learning the right things. If I'd had that feedback and training earlier, I don't know that I'd have made it on the tour but I sure would have been a lot better than I was and I might have had a chance. Looking back upon it now, it was very clear that I did not have a chance. I could have practiced for 95 years, practicing the wrong things, and I would have just been a better mediocre player.

Q: You've had a fair share of pro golfers pass through your tutelage, what do they have that the rest of us don't have?

A: I believe that they are all good athletes. You can't be out there without some athletic talent but the men that I have worked with, talk about major winners. The first one I ever worked with who won a major was Tom Kite and he's the worst athlete of the whole group.

Q: Yeah, Tom Kite and the word *athlete* are not often in the same sentence….

A: But he's learned. He became a great short game player, a reasonably good putter and a fairly good ball striker. And he's gone from there with great determination and great repetition and great devotion. He's very bright and he's become a great golfer.

But his coordination? He doesn't hold a candle to Ben Crenshaw. He can't begin to carry his bag, but he's actually had a better career than Ben. He's won more money, and he's been a better player.

• •

ON THE VALUE OF DIAGNOSTIC GEAR AT PELZ GOLF INSTITUTE:

"Probably a million dollars. I use lasers, accelerometers, strain gauges but there is no commercial equipment available for what I use. I have to first figure out what do I want to measure? Then how do I measure it and finally what do I have to build special so that it doesn't offend, interrupt or distract the golfer?"

• •

The people I have worked with over the years who have won majors include Steve Elkington, Lee Janzen, V.J. Singh, Mike Weir. These guys have come to our school, worked hard, and I don't believe that they are better or worse athletes than thousands and thousands of others. Now they're good—I'm not saying that they're not—but they're not God-given talents placed on earth.

Q: Okay, so how does it happen?

A: Well, you learn. You learn with the proper feedback, whether it comes from a video camera, from a teacher, from your own practice device or from your own vision and attention. It's all out there. There's nothing magical about hitting a golf ball from point A to point B. But there is an awful lot of physics involved. And if you don't understand it, and somebody is sitting there and telling you that you need to put more weight toward your front foot during the middle of your swing, and if that's wrong—then you could do that the rest of your life, and it's not going to help. In fact, it's going to hurt.

It's a combination of being a good enough athlete so that you can, in fact, be in good enough shape, although Craig Stadler proves that you don't have to be a decathlete to be a great player. But you have to have a certain amount of strength, a certain amount of health and a certain coordination of your mind and eyes and body but you don't have to be a physical specimen. You don't.

I have seen Lee Janzen improve. I've seen Steve Elkington improve. I have seen Mike Weir get better and better and better. But they focus on the right things and in the right way. They work on their bodies to make it more capable of performing. I think great champions are built. I don't think they are born.

Q: That's good to know. I try three times a week to take 15 minutes, maybe a half hour, to stop at a golf course and go to their practice green and just putz around with the putter or wedge. It helps, particularly just from the fringe because you're going to miss greens.

A: You bet it helps. Absolutely. A friend of mine, Tom Purtzer [five-time PGA Tour winner]. He's not a close personal friend but I've known Tom for 25 years. He might be the best athlete I've ever seen. He's on the Champions Tour now. And he's won $250,000 to $1 million every year. He's probably a better athlete than Sevie Ballesteros, who was great. He just has these magical hands and this incredible athletic ability to do things. Yet neither one was ever the greatest player in the world, because that's not what it's all about. It is athletic but it's also timing and rhythm and physics. You've got to have the ball in the right place. You've got to be accelerating. You've got to be doing a lot of things. What makes golf so great to me is that you can learn it.

Q: When you sit there watching any of the guys you named on TV and notice they're still doing something you showed them, you must get those "Ah-hah, yes!" moments?

A: Absolutely! That's where I get my thrills. You can't imagine the excitement for me. Since V.J. Singh came to our school, he's won two majors, The Masters and the PGA. And Phil just won his first major, The Masters, and almost won his second a few weeks ago. It is a tremendous thrill. But it's not just Phil Mickelson and V.J. Singh.

We have an alumnus from our school—and you know enough about golf that you will appreciate this—he's a 12 handicap and he's 83-years-old. When he came to our school, he was 81. He just wrote us a letter that said: *Mr. Pelz, I want to tell you how excited I am. At age 83, I just played in this tournament that I've been playing in for many many years. I have never won it before. I played in it 35 times, and I won it this year for the first time in my life. But that's not what I'm excited about. In the third round of a four round tournament, I shot the best score of my life and in the fourth round, I beat it!*

He credited his short game, which was apparently phenomenal for that tournament.

I get goose pimples just sitting here talking to you about that story. Here's an 83-year-old playing the best game of his life. Seems to me that I ought to be able to do it at 70.

Q: Advice for people who are thinking about taking up the game of golf, either for personal or professional reasons. What do you say to them?

A: Start close to the hole and do it with good teachers.

2

Grow

Larry Bossidy, *Honeywell*

Larry Bossidy, former vice chairman of General Electric and former chief executive of Allied Signal, believes that a successful company must embrace a discipline of execution in all its core processes. One of the world's most respected and successful executives, he is also the former Chairman of the Board of Honeywell International Inc., where he led 115,000 workers in 100 countries.

Question: Are there some generational challenges ahead for companies—the expectations and work ethic of the twenty-somethings and thirty-somethings now in the work force?

Answer: You could've asked that same question 20 years

ago and you'd have the same response today. Sure, generations are different, but I go around to business schools, asI did when I was running Honeywell. I talk to lots of folks, and the amount of talent that is coming through is just remarkable. This generation, while different in some respects, is very talented. I don't think we face any more of a transitional challenge today than we ever have.

Q: The Employment Policy Foundation takes a look at demographic trending and suggests that there won't be enough people out there 20 years from now for companies to achieve peak productivity—that there will be a shortfall of talent and people in raw numbers.

A: I think that's a lot of baloney. These same people have been saying that for years. I don't believe it. You could argue that we're graduating too many people from our colleges and universities than too few. Obviously, we'll always need people, but we are generating an enormous number of educated people every year, and a larger percentage every year are people from foreign countries. We'll always try to get a better work force. It is something you strive for on a continuous basis, but I'm not the least bit concerned that we lack the necessary people to keep this economy going at a vibrant pace.

Q: Can you point out what the three or five critical elements are for an organization to get things done?

A: I think first of all you have to have a discipline of creating, energizing, and sustaining an integrated business system of implementation, as opposed to just announcing strategies. I think it has to be the primary job of a leader. If the leader isn't involved in understanding the significance of execution, the rest of the organization won't be involved. I think that if you can establish such a culture—one that takes great pride in its accomplishments—then you can differentiate yourself among your competitors. That's the first thing.

What else is important? There are three major processes that have to provide substantial yields. One is the people process—their appraisal, their rotation, their coaching, efforts that develop quality people. That must be done intensely. Then there's a strategic process where you make sure you're wrestling with the issues confronting the business and resolving them. Finally, there's an operational process where you prepare a budget and then you measure against your performance on the budget. All three should be linked. That's the groundwork for a performance-oriented company.

Q: One of the toughest issues for a company is to determine what product or service is going to have an emerging demand. An existing demand is pretty obvious. How can firms find an emerging demand in that timeless supply-and-demand equation?

A: Businesses must look at the environment they are in. Get a lot of information with respect to customer desires, wants, and needs, and then try to structure a product or service in keeping with what those demands are. You're not always going to be right because times change, customers change. But nonetheless, that's the way you go about it. And if your batting average in anticipating change is pretty good, you're successful.

Q: Having the right people is critical.

A: It is the most important thing you do in business. You've got to get the right people and if you don't have the right people, you've got to change them. If you don't get that right, nothing else works. And you want to have people who pay attention to what's going on on the outside. A lot of companies worry too much about what's going on in the inside, their own internal politics, as opposed to making sure they understand what customers want and paying attention to external clues as to how to modify their business.

Q: As you look back on your tenure and time at Honeywell, name the one thing that you think you did right.

A: I think we got good people. We got a lot of them. I like to think I did more than one thing right.

Q: Go ahead and stretch that list out a little bit.

A: I think quality people were challenged to improve. We

provided a good concise strategy that everybody understood and a discipline to meet our commitment. I think it takes time, but once you reach that point, a momentum kicks in and that has great value.

Q: Momentum is a funny one. It comes and goes.
A: It does, and you know, it's always there. It may be working against you. It may be working for you. But it's always there. I also think if you have a performance-oriented company, a company with a history of execution, a number of things will be present. Look at P&G. It's a company that has been stumbling around out there for many years. There have been a lot of good years. There have been a lot of disappointing years. But I think you see, with the new CEO, that they have found a way to make things happen, a way to get things done. I think it's having an impact on the whole company in a positive and persuasive way.

They had a CEO by the name of Durk Jager. He was probably doing all the right things but did not communicate in a particularly insightful way. Two things are important in business: deciding what to do—and oftentimes, that's easy—and then deciding how to do it. That's tough. There is sometimes too much time and attention paid on the former. Not enough time and attention paid on the latter.

Q: When you see performance-oriented companies, what are the common traits?
A: One, the leader knows the business so he can knowledgably participate in the important decisions. He also knows the key people—their hopes, their aspirations, their strengths and their shortcomings. He can participate in the key personnel decisions. If you're running a company and are not intimately familiar with the people you promote, I don't know how you can be successful. Remember, there are a lot of people who see the world the way they wish it was and not the way it is.

You have to be realistic. You have to set clear goals. Simplicity and focus are the marks of a good organization, as opposed to complexity, that is—laying out a hundred goals where people have no idea about what's important and what's not.

Good companies reward the doers; they make sure the organization understands that those who are being rewarded are the people who get things done, as opposed to the philosophers who wander around the halls.

Performance-oriented companies coach their people so they get better. They are willing to have a conversation with someone who tells them that they have three or four shortcomings. They realize they have the potential to overcome them. It's a discussion that must be held in a candid way.

And finally, good leaders contain their own egos. They don't get caught up going to Washington for a black-tie dinner every Wednesday night. They realize their job is to run the company, and that's where they spend most of their time. Every time a CEO gets fired, almost invariably the reason that is given is that they weren't able to execute their plan.

3

✸Niche

Sam Zell, *Financier*

Chicago financier and billionaire Samuel Zell is a modern-day Atlas of industry with a roster of companies that reaches around the globe. Zell is also known for his eccentricities — more likely to wear a Loony Toons shirt to his office on the Chicago River than worsted wool. Other days, he dresses in sweats. Transportation to his office is usually on one of his half-dozen motorcycles. And he knows how to have off-duty fun, too. When he throws a party, it may be a 24-hour affair that spans Chicago to New York to London to Paris on a private jet with stops at buildings his company owns along the way. He takes an annual two-week motorcycle jaunt with friends, the Zell's Angels — trips that include a mechanic and a chase truck for repairs. Excursions may begin in Spain and end in Nice.

One year it's the Alps of Slovenia, the next year it's the Balkans. No primitive camp-outs under the stars for this crew, either; it's five-star all the way.

Zell started out in business by buying apartment buildings upon his graduation from the University of Michigan. In recent years, his business interests have ranged from office space to fiber optics, from mattresses to household products companies, from senior citizen housing sites to radio stations. His interests ebb and flow with the twin tides of value and opportunity.

Question: You have the reputation of being a "vulture investor," the...
Answer: Grave Dancer?

Q: Yes, but I understand you are paying some fairly steep prices for some office buildings now. You're no longer making low-ball offers?
A: Oh, I don't think we've ever done that. I really don't. I think we are cold-cocked realists. When your market is 25 percent vacant, and your building is 50 percent vacant and you're seeking to sell it, what else can I do but make you an offer based upon what I think it's worth? We bought the BP building in Cleveland, a huge building. They put it on the market. That was a building I wanted to own. We pre-empted the bidding and bought it.

CDs in the Changer

Experience the Divine by Bette Midler

America IV: The Man Comes Around by Johnny Cash

There were lots of reasons. Rarely are reasons limited to the specific asset. When you look at something like Equity Office, which is the largest owner of office space in the United States [Zell is the chairman of the board of trustees], we determine a building's value by how it fits our portfolio. So I don't think it's fair to even make a judgment to "value" because really, it's value to whom, and under what circumstances.

Q: Let's switch to radio. In 1997, the average station sold for $8.03 million. It dropped to $5 million in 1998. In 1996, about $14.3 billion worth of radio stations changed hands. In 1997, about $18 billion changed hands. In 1998, $9 billion. There seems to be a trend there that maybe it was time to get out of radio. Is that why you cashed out of radio?

A: I think the statistics that you just quoted reflect the fact that in February 1996, Congress passed telecom deregulation. That created an extraordinary period of consolidation. That consolidation was primarily finished by the end of 1997. So it would frankly scare me if the numbers went the other way. But I don't necessarily agree that there's any correlation between the completion of the consolidation phase and the prospects of radio going forward. My view on radio revenue is that the analogy is probably very similar to the railroad business.

· ·
BOOKS ON THE NIGHTSTAND

"I'm an avid escapist reader who consumes a couple of books a week...none of which I remember. This is the current candidate."

Exile **by Allan Folsom**
· ·

For years, the truckers ate the railroads' lunch and the railroads ended up getting smaller and smaller percentages of the railroad freight. The railroads woke up one day and said, "We have to do something about this." And that led to the creation of container trains and efficiency and, in effect, the railroads have been taking business back from the trucks. Well, if you look at the radio business prior to 1996, it was highly fragmented. It had consumptive competition. In other words, it was self-destructive competition, all kinds of people owning all kinds of stations, and nobody had a big enough piece to make a difference.

The consolidation that occurred after the Telecommunications Act ['96] made radio a much more viable media if for no other reason than that advertisers could go to

Jacor or Clear Channel or Chancellor or CBS and make one deal across the country. In the old days when companies were limited to owning 17 stations, you had a cluster that owned big-market stations, and a cluster that owned middle markets and small markets. In many cases, the biggest radio station in the market had 6-8 percent share. That's a hell of a lot different from being offered the opportunity to sign on with Jacor in Cincinnati, where they had a 40 percent market share. That made radio a much more attractive media. Looking ahead, I think radio is going to get a higher percentage of the advertising dollar.

Q: Will there ever be a return on investment to match yours in the former Jacor—a $73 million investment and four years later you cash out of Clear Channel for about $1.3 billion cash? That's an incredible return.

A: That's unlikely in the radio business. But other businesses? Quite possible. All kinds of consolidations are possible.

I think much of this is a result of a changed view of antitrust law. If you remember back to the late 1960s, regulators were taking on companies solely based on their size. In those days, they never considered foreign competition. In the enlightened '90s, where foreign competition was much more relevant, size itself was not bad. I think there are lots of businesses where more efficiency is possible and the ability to extract redundancies is also very real.

Q: So is everybody wearing blue jeans in here today? [Zell is wearing a shirt with a monogrammed Sylvester the Cat above the pocket.]

A: Absolutely. It's really simple. If you're really good at what you do and you dress funny, you're eccentric. If you're not so good at what you do and you dress funny, you're a schmuck. So our motivation here has always been to be extraordinarily good at what we do, so therefore we can wear whatever we want. We've been doing that for 30 years.

Q: Back to real estate. Are you going to have all your office buildings wired for broadband Internet?

A: Yeah, as a matter of fact, I invested in a company called Allied Riser Corp., and ARC is basically in the business of putting fiber-optic backbones into buildings, and they are selling services to tenants on a per-desktop basis.

Q: What would you tell other companies about how to get highly-regarded and competent employees?
A: We have been very fortunate in our ability to attract and, more importantly, to keep good people. Number one, we are constantly a growing entity. And because we have such diverse interests, there is rarely a time where some part of our world is not growing very rapidly and creating opportunity.
Number two, we have always been focused on a meritocracy. Consequently, people who join our organization are measured by what they contribute, not necessarily how old they are or where they are in the pecking order.
Number three, I'd like to think that the leadership I provide is quite different because I'm very accessible. I really, really believe in the 11th Commandment.

Q: What is that?
A: Thou shalt not take thyself seriously. And I think that under that set of circumstances, we are able to keep and recruit good people.

Q: OK, you have five minutes with a President, whoever that may be, what would you say?
A: Globalization is not a fad, but a reality. The interlocking of the world from an informational point of view has enormous implications upon everything we do. And what makes America great and what makes America the leading power in the world is our creation of an open environment. So I would encourage him to advocate less regulation and less impairment to everybody's ability to function. Can you imagine if there were regulations on the creation of Internet companies, what would have happened? Or what wouldn't have happened? It's very interesting that the U.S. is way ahead of the rest of the world on the Internet. A lot of that has to do with the fact that it's easy access—a society that encourages innovation, encourages challenge.

Q: What advice would you give to a college graduate who wants to become another Sam Zell?

A: I think what I would tell an aggressive person is, first and foremost—make no little plans. Go for greatness; nobody makes it with half efforts, and nobody succeeds without pain, without extraordinary effort. And although it's a cliche, the long-term investor always wins.

4

�֎Audacity

Jerry Springer

Long before the glamour, the bright lights of Broadway, the notoriety and the scorn, talk-show host Jerry Springer was just another rookie city councilman in Cincinnati. He was earning $8,000 a year from city hall and living in an $85 a month apartment in the blue-collar neighborhood of Westwood. Unlike other council members, Springer was an activist, and one of his first missions was to get the city jail closed and a new one built.

During some summers, temperatures in the sprawling castle-like jail were in the 90's and stayed that way for days on end. There was no running water in cells. Inmates had buckets to use at night instead of toilets. There was only natural lighting in the cells and not much of that, either. Prisoners were locked in one by one at night. It was a firetrap. Nobody much cared that the Civil War-era jail had been obsolete for decades. Let 'em rot in there, was the attitude. It's punishment, after all.

And then came Springer. Reared in New York City and a graduate of Tulane University and the Northwestern University School of Law, Springer was a campus organizer for Bobby Kennedy before arriving in Cincinnati to work as an associate-minion at a law firm. But he hated the drudgery of law and ran for city council as a Democrat in one of the most conservative cities in the nation. He won. One of his first acts was to arrange to get himself locked up in the jail to get a firsthand impression of its misery.

But when a local TV station broadcast the rookie council member Springer in jail, inmates watching the show began to grumble. Springer, eating dinner in the jail, watched as the grumbling grew to an eruption, everybody looking at him; a scared, long-haired Jewish guy from New York City with a funny accent and big city ways.

This time, he felt, he'd really done it. Surrounded by angry and annoyed scoundrels, drunks, wife-beaters, drug dealers, check-kiters and all manner of thugs, Springer had no choice. He climbed up on a dining table and started to talk.

Question: So what did you tell the inmates?

Answer: Well, I told them that nobody should have to live under these conditions, that it certainly was not going to rehabilitate anybody, and that I was not trying to get anyone inside in trouble but that I was trying to figure out how to make it better. I told them that I was not there to help anybody get out. Their lawyers and the justice system would handle that. We knew we had to have people incarcerated. I wanted to find the best way to do that and still protect and serve the community. I told them that this was the United States of America and that the conditions inside represented cruel and unusual punishment. I told them prisoners should have adequate toilet facilities, adequate living space.

Q: Where is that activism in politics today? What happened to it?

A: There is activism but not among politicians. There's very little of that. But activism is out there. It's as if activists are so turned off by traditional politics that they've all gone their separate ways. There are a few who stayed within the system, but the system is compromised. And it's compromised by a little thing that gets very little attention because it sounds boring. What has compromised political debate in America is redistricting.

There are very few places in America where there is any political debate anymore. The communities are either overwhelmingly Democrat or overwhelmingly Republican. You can have a national debate, but it never takes place in Congress because every Congressman knows that there is no reason to discuss or compromise because their district is probably behind them anyway so they've got to toe the line. You'll never get a big liberal out of the First District of Ohio. And you won't get a conservative out of the inner city of Cleveland. So no discussion takes place. Everybody is safe.

• •

CDs in the Changer

Dedicated to You by Joni James

Profile(The Best of Emmylou Harris) by Emmylou Harris

Columbia Records 1958-1986 by Johnny Cash

Remembering the 50's by Various Artists

All Killer, No Filler: The Anthology by Jerry Lee Lewis

• •

And it's exacerbated by the media and their talking–head shows, where to be on and discuss anything, you have to be clearly on one side or the other. You can't be down the middle. I get calls to appear on some of these shows—I'm not on a lot—and they ask me, which position are you going to take? "Oh, you're to the left-of-center? Good, we'll find someone from the right-of-center."

There's no give-and-take in the halls of Congress because

no one needs to, that is, no one has a constituency that they have to explain anything to. I think that until we change this process to one where people who are elected are required to work with all the constituencies—and not go down the left road or the right road. Until we get away from the ideological separation, we're not going to have any discussion at all.

And our political conventions are so canned. We know we're being duped. They explain during the shows what they're going to be doing. So we go out there and applaud, knowing that it's part of a plan. The Republicans know that there's a middle band of voters so they only have speakers that appeal to them.

We know that's the plan: get the middle vote. The speeches all talk about moderation. You have Schwarzenegger up there —God bless him—but the Republicans in power disagree with every social position he takes. So the rule is don't talk about any social position. Talk about coming to America, and how great that is, and "I love free enterprise." But don't talk about your position on abortion. Don't talk about gays.

There's no room right now for activism in institutional politics. So it takes place outside—on the fringes. How much discussion did we get from the networks about the protests that took place on the streets of New York City during the Republican convention? None. Absolutely none. And the media has been totally co-opted by the political establishment.

Q: Flash back to 1980. You're a councilman in Cincinnati —one of dozens of ambitious council members from a big city in Ohio—and you decide to run for governor. That's pretty audacious right there. You get a list of private plane owners, and then you meet with people on the list: "Hello, I'm Jerry Springer, I'm running for governor, and I'd like your support." People would meet you and write a check? Just like that? Whose idea was that list?

A: It was my idea. I didn't have any money, and I was unknown. I wasn't going to get any institutional money, so I had to figure out who was I really trying to reach, anyway? I was in favor of changing what was going on, but I had nobody to go to. People in the Democratic Party were backing Celeste and Brown, as they should have, because they were more experienced. So I started thinking: where were our resources going to come from?

So, I figured to go with people who were not part of the power structure but had all the talents, understood success and knew how to make something work. They were the entrepreneurial class but weren't yet part of the establishment and maybe, for personality reasons, would never become part of the establishment. I went to them and said, "Look, we're at a point in our lives, why are we always being told what to do? This is our world, our state. You're smart. Look what you've done with your business. Let's fix this state." It's not all that different from what I'm saying now when I go around. We're in horrible shape. We know it. Don't tell me "Democrat", "Republican"—we're in horrible shape.

I asked them, "If this was your job to fix it, how would you fix it? Don't give me ideology. How would you fix it?" Someone wants a job. That's not ideology. Get them a job. Let's come up with ideas on how to get them jobs. I was just trying to look for outward signs of success. So, if you own a plane and your dad didn't give it to you—and most [dads] didn't because even wealthy dads weren't of the generation that owned planes—then that was a sign of someone who was entrepreneurial, someone who was out there on their own.

Q: How much did you raise?

A: At that time it was quite a bit of money—$3 million altogether, not just from the list of plane owners. Probably $1 million from plane owners. It came from people who had discretionary income, and there was a rule. The rule was—and I also knew it would work—that if you gave, you would never do business with the state and you couldn't get a job from me. It was very effective to tell them straight up because it almost put them on the defensive. If they then didn't give, it was almost like, well, they were looking for something. It was the only way to do it. If not, you're going to be owned forever, and why live like that? Why get into politics?

So I said, "Here's the rule. You're giving because you have a wonderful, successful life. This is like you're giving to your church. You're doing this because you believe in it. You want life to be better. It can't be that you're giving to make more money. Make money in business. Don't make money through government."

And this generation really understood that. Let's face it, a guy who owns a plane isn't looking for a job. It was the right thing to do but it wasn't very difficult and I wasn't real courageous. But that was the rule: give me money, there's nothing material in it for you.

Q: Careers have pivot points. Was that yours because it showed you the career potential of media? You went right from politics into being a news anchor and finally into a gig as a talk show host.

A: Well, it's all hindsight. I was offered my first job in media but I never thought for a minute about being in media. After I lost my primary race for governor, I went to Hilton Head the next day. I was going to be there for a week. And that week, I got calls from three different Cincinnati television stations. Now, how did that happen? Probably word got out that one station was looking for me so the others came talking to me about employment. Both wanted me to be a political commentator to anchoring the news. So I decided to go with WLW-TV 5 because they were at the bottom, and I figured I could learn.

Q: You have quite a life. One night at some London soiree with celebrities, and the next night, literally the next night, you're a continent away in Fairfield County, Ohio, at a rubber chicken banquet for local Democrats.

A: Yes, I have a strange life. And I've been blessed. What I've found is there's no difference between wealthy people and others except for the clothes and their command of the English language. And the only difference between England and America is the accent. I noticed that a lot because I'm back and forth all the time. And when you look at younger people, aged 16 to 30 and get 10 from England, 10 from America, 10 from South Africa, 10 from Italy and 10 from France, those kids will talk about the same things: dating, sports, school, clothing, whether they have a job, and what CDs they're listening to. I'm telling you there is no difference. The only difference between people in any society is that some people elevate themselves because they have more money, they dress better, and they speak their language better. Otherwise, they are all the same. It's not a cliché—it's true.

Q: Your talk show is a magnet for criticism for showing the worst of American life. It strikes me that it's always been little more than a camera on reality.

A: The people on my show don't act any differently than wealthy people. The example I always give is that an English professor at Harvard comes home one evening and finds his wife in bed with a neighbor. He's not going to say, "Forsooth my dear, look what I have found." He's going to say, "Get the f— out of here," and start yelling at the wife, storm out. What is different?

Now what our show does, which is admittedly a stupid show—now, it's not aimed at me, but in college, I guess, I would have enjoyed it—what our show does is it shows people who we're not used to seeing on television. The anger is not the issue.

When people get upset and ask, "How can you put that on television?" Well, it's because they're only used to seeing upper-middle class, white people on television. That is American television: upper-middle class and white. It's all *Friends* and *Seinfeld* and *Frazier*, and if you're black, then you'd better be a doctor living and working in the suburbs like Cosby otherwise you're relegated to WB or UPN. It's all the same. Even the news is all the same. If you are a black anchor, you can't speak Ebonics, you better speak white, suburban English. So it's all the same.

And then along comes our show, and for the first time we're airing people you see every day walking down any street in America, whether it's rural or big city. We see these people every single day. And what they talk about happens every single day. But we had never seen it on television before and that offended some peoples' sensibilities.

Q: Okay, these folks are out there and, as a result, you've managed to channel hundreds of millions of dollars

in advertising revenues to the show. It changed the daytime TV paradigm.

A: Advertisers always go where the audience is. Our advertisers may be different. But ultimately, it's a science. They do the survey work, the polls, who's watching, what do they buy? And that's the business.

Now, this uppity stuff at some of the networks, how they would never do what we're doing. Well, two years later, here comes reality television on the networks every single night. It's like our show with one exception; the people on those shows are beautiful. That's the only difference. They are sleeping with each other. They are showing greed. They are arguing. But they're beautiful.

It's the same with soap operas. Every dysfunction in the world is on a soap opera, but the people are drop-dead gorgeous. What's offensive to the pundits is that they are not used to seeing someone on television who isn't beautiful. The American Idol show—who the hell wins? People who look the best.

By the way, if you lived my life, you'd have no idea that the show was controversial. That's the difference between what a critic writes—and that's their job—and what people think when they see me in person on the street. I mean, there is no controversy. None, ever. I can't think of a nasty experience. I never get, "How dare you run that show."

Q: Never a fourth grade teacher wagging her finger at you?

A: Oh, no. Never! This is what I get. God's truth, the teacher will come up, "Could you please sign this? Could I have this picture? My class will love it."

In real life, do you think anyone on this planet goes to sleep at night thinking, "Oh, The Jerry Springer show! Oh, what's the world coming to?" And yet you read those who criticize the show, you'd think people all over America were having chest pains because of the show. Are there people who hate the show? Of course—but they don't watch it.

There are lots of things I don't like, but I've never hated anyone because of a television show. You can hate a politician because they can send you to war or cause you to lose your job. In television, I have never felt the animosity that I felt when I was in politics. Then you're talking about things that people really care about. Nobody cares about television. People love the show or they don't watch it.

Q: You mentioned South Africa. How long does it take to get from Atlanta to Johannesburg?
A: It takes 19 hours and is the longest non-stop flight in the world.

Q: You know that for a fact, because you funded a talk show there with the proceeds going to AIDS research. Not many people know that about you.
A: Once a month, I went there to tape four shows. I'm not doing it right now but I did it for a year. I don't get a penny. It costs me money. In fact it costs quite a bit of money. But what the show raises through commercials goes to fight AIDS. I don't know how much it has raised, but it's a lot. I paid the cost of my own travel and put up 50 percent of the cost of the show—about $500,000.

Q: There's an element of Mickey as the Sorcerer's Apprentice to this. You're just one man. You're dumping the buckets but the flood is coming. You're just one guy. Why would you think you can make an impact on a problem so big?
A: I'm just like anybody. You do what you can. Why does a person give to charity? You know your contribution won't cure cancer but you're one of many. This was something that I was in a position to do something about. So I decided to help raise money by what I do in my business. That doesn't make me wonderful.

Most people I know that if there's a hurricane or other disaster, they give. People give at their church. Celebrities just get attention because they're known. I'm not Mother Theresa, but everybody wants a life that is productive. Most of us were raised that way. I'm unique in that I don't have financial issues in my life because of the show. So I ask, "What's the best use of my time? Charitable endeavors."

Q: You either are or are not running for governor of Ohio.
A: I might. Honestly, I wake up in the morning and go, *Arrrghhhhh.*

Q: Are you telling me you still have that crisis of "What am I going to be when I grow up?"
A: I've said that by the time I'm 90, I'm going to make a decision about what I want to be. I want to do what is most productive. There are tons of decisions that have to be made. Instinctively, my cares are more political. It is the one area of my life where I think I have a gift. I really can be a good communicator. That's what I can do. Even before all these years in television. Somehow, people relate when I talk. They see authenticity. So that is a gift. And I know I can do that. I can stand before a crowd and say, "Follow me. This is how we can fix it."

When I came to Cincinnati, which was—next to San Diego—the most conservative city in America, here I was, a long-haired liberal New York Jew coming to Cincinnati. In a couple of years, I was mayor, even after a scandal—[he paid a prostitute with a check, apologized and resigned from council and was re-elected]—so I know I can communicate. And it's a gift. I know I can give money to causes, but other people can give money, too. Is that the best use of my gift of communication? Hopefully, I'm smart enough to have some good ideas, so why not do this in a political arena? That is the absolute truth about what I think about almost all the time. So I'm moving as if I'm making a run for governor, and I probably will.

Q: Not many people know this but you're something of a policy wonk, aren't you?
A: Yeah.

Q: When you have nothing to do, you read, what, the *National Review*?
A: Well, what I read all the time is *The New Republic,*

Nation and *The Weekly Standard*. So I get the left and the right. And I read either *Time* or *Newsweek* every week. I get my fix of *The New York Times* every morning, which is how I got addicted to Starbucks. In so many places, it's hard to get *The New York Times*. But when you're traveling, if there's a Starbucks, you'll find *The New York Times*. Now I'm addicted to Starbucks. And probably for political reasons I shouldn't be doing that. I always get the mocha with cream.

Q: Talk about public education. What needs to be done?

A: Overwhelmingly: early childhood, early childhood, early childhood, early childhood education. And it should start at birth, not at three years old or even two. With a lot of these teenaged mothers, you almost have to have someone in that delivery room. Someone who is just being around, someone who can provide help two days a week, someone who can work with the mother and work with the child. Someone who can stimulate them, who can come one hour on Tuesday afternoons, who can help the mother develop a habit so that every day the child can look at this, or play with that. It's kind of like a counselor.

Q: Would this program be like a Peace Corps?

A: I don't know who would do it but it could be. What I do know is that we have to start the debate so that there is an emphasis on early childhood education, so that that child, starting in the first grade, is ready to compete with suburban kids.

Here's what happens. First, when the suburban kid goes to school, they are already at this level **[his left hand is held high]** and the kid who is either from a rural poverty area or city urban poverty area is so far behind **[right hand is very low]** because of the chaos of poverty in their home.

We are kidding ourselves when we say, "Well, if the teacher would just do it this way." Who are you kidding? That kid shows up at school and from the first day doesn't know the name of his parents, thinks they're named Mom and Dad. They don't know where they live, the address. Nothing.

There's no stimulation at home. Not because they're bad parents but because they're overwhelmed. They're up all night or one parent is gone. There's nothing happening in that household. That kid starts out so far behind they can't achieve any success in school, so therefore, like any child, they don't like what they're not good at. We need to start with early childhood education. It's vital.

• •

Books on the Nightstand

Adams and Jefferson: The Tumultuous Election (Pivotal Moments in American History) **by John Ferling**

Bushworld **by Maureen Dowd**

What Went Wrong: The Clash Between Islam and Modernity in the Middle East **by Bernard Lewis**

• •

Two, we need smaller classroom size in these troubled school districts. No more than 15 kids in a classroom. So now you've hit the problem two ways. One, you get them from birth with early childhood education. Two, they go to school and get real small classroom size so they can get needed attention and feel success.

And three, you cap it all off with free college tuition for any student who majors in math or science, as long as they agree to stay in Ohio after graduation and teach math or science for at least four years. You can play with that. Maybe you add nursing because there's a great need for nurses. Or maybe you say that from now on, anyone who gets state aid for college in Ohio has to stay in Ohio for a couple of years. We have great colleges in Ohio. But people graduate, and then they leave.

Q: What would you do about economic development?
A: This is a broad view because we're working on details now. I see health care as an economic development concern beyond the obvious moral and health issues involved. Looking beyond off–shoring and out–sourcing, it's clear that Ohio companies can have trouble competing. A major cost of hiring

an employee now is health insurance—more than a third of the cost. But what if we took that off the bargaining table? So the overall plan would look something like this:

You pass a law that everyone in Ohio has to have health insurance, just like if you have a car you have to have auto insurance. That's the law. You have to have it. For those who can't afford it, you subsidize it. A number of things would flow from that. [One,] everyone would have health insurance. Two, companies that couldn't afford it would get a subsidy. Three, all of a sudden employers would say, "Let's go to Ohio because it's a great place to do business. Look how cheap it is to do business there."

Not all employers would drop their health plans because they would want to compete for the best employees. So a Procter & Gamble, for instance, would continue to have great benefits for their employees because they would want the best people to come to them and not go to Colgate.

Small businesses that couldn't afford to hire additional people because of the health insurance costs, they all of a sudden are in the game. Now you have employers staying in Ohio, new employers flocking to Ohio because it's so cheap to do business here and, because you have more people working in Ohio, you now have more taxpayers and that would increase the revenue that you now collect—not by raising taxes but by having more taxes. That money is used to subsidize the cost of health insurance.

Finally, with all these millions of Ohioans who are now part of this health insurance plan, I would then go as governor to the insurance companies and say, "I have these seven million customers. What's your best price? Nah, I'll go to the next one. What's your best price?" So you can now have competition because the pool is so large. All of a sudden, the cost of health insurance goes down for everybody.

So what have you done? One, everyone has health insurance. Two, you've lowered the cost of health insurance because the pool is so large. And three, those who can't afford it can get it subsidized. Four, you have higher employment than you've ever had in Ohio, reversing the outflow of jobs. Suddenly there's an inflow of jobs. And you get all the things that come about as a result: economic development, jobs, people fixing up their communities.

That's the overall plan. It could be magic for Ohio. And what's more, I may decide to go to the governor of Michigan and Indiana and get a regional thing going. Now it's 15 million to 20 million customers to take to the insurance companies. You leave it in the private sector so it's not the government running it, but we're the customer. Now that's a big idea.

Q: Did you think all this up?
A: Yeah, yeah. So, what I've done is I'm convening some really, really smart people on health care and insurance. This is the issue I have given them, and I said work out the numbers for me. We may have to tweak here and tweak there. We probably have to take catastrophic insurance out of the mix, which would also drive the price down. There are things we can do. With this plan, companies can afford to pay higher wages and hire more people.

There are so many pluses that come about as a result of this. Right now, we can't compete with European companies because European companies don't have to provide health insurance for their workers. It puts us back on the playing field. This would only get passed by someone who doesn't have to worry about the political consequences. I figured it could be my legacy because I don't care about a political career. If I can do this, I'll serve my term and get the hell out.

Q: Your career, your life, has had a lot of twists and turns.
A: I've been blessed—and I would say that 99 percent of success is that and luck. You could take what every one of us who has been successful has done and [you will find] there are other people who have done the exact same thing and they are not successful. That's why I'm saying it's not like, "Well, here's the formula." Whatever it is, tons of people are doing the same thing.

Now, it is true that if you look at all successful people you'll find a common denominator. But the corollary of that is not to say that if you do this, you will be successful. When I say 99 percent is luck, that means it's a gift from God. You have to start from this place: I didn't decide to be born. That's a gift from God. I didn't decide to have great parents. That's a gift from God. It wasn't my decision to have a decent brain. That's a gift from God.

All these things that you find in successful people, it's all a gift. Put a successful person in a room, cut through the bullshit and ask, and you'll find this is true: most were just plain lucky.

5

✸Risk

Tami Longaberger, *The Longaberger Company*

To find the greatest number of artisans in the world under one roof, a traveler does not journey to artist enclaves in Sedona, Costa Rica or Europe. Instead, they head into the heartland of America to The Longaberger Company in Dresden, Ohio, where 1,000 people twist, weave and nail thin strips of maple into an astounding variety of baskets. Some baskets have sleek contemporary lines, others are as timeless in their design as a 19th century "Currier and Ives" picnic. All are miniature pieces of architecture and each is signed by the artisan who created it.

The pride in those signatures represents the dream of the late Dave Longaberger, a former owner of the Dresden IGA

Foodliner, a small–town grocery store.

One day Longaberger followed his curiosity and ended up building a basket empire. His daughter, Tami Longaberger, is now chief executive of the company, which has posted annual revenues of more than $1 billion and employs more than 4,000 people. But before the company leadership role, before the billions in revenues, Tami Longaberger was just another high school graduate-to-be who was pulling a Friday night shift behind the cash register at a grocery store in a crossroads Ohio town.

Question: Tell me about those days behind that cash register in that grocery store when you were 16.

Answer: On Friday nights, many times, it would only be the younger folks working in the grocery store. I remember my Dad forbade me from being back in the meat department because we were the only ones working—there were no adults and he was afraid somebody would get hurt. There was a heated unit—used to shrink wrap the meat. We found out you could turn that on, get some aluminum foil and grill a couple of hamburgers for dinner.

Q: Nice…
A: And I don't think my Dad knew I did that.

Q: Duties? Stocking shelves?
A: And running the cash register. Wednesday night was stock night. That's when the truck came in from Navarre. It was a two-register store—before scanning units—so check-out was by hand.

Q: Did you like it?
A: Yeah, I did. I worked three days a week from [age] 14 until I graduated from high school. My dad taught me a lot of things and mostly it was by on-the-job training, just by doing. It wasn't by lecture, although, in the car, just like any other dad I suppose, he wanted to guide and shape me.

The lessons that stayed with me were from the restaurant, from the grocery store, from the drug store, and from watching my dad put all those businesses at risk to make the basket business a success. In challenging times like we're working through now, you look back to some of the things you've learned, which got you to this point. Certainly working hard, determination, and basically doing something—trying something—don't sit around and wait for it to change on it's own.

"Do something." That was my father's mantra.

Q: About half the company revenues come from selling products other than baskets. Moving the company into non-basket areas like ironworks, plastic liners, pottery, that's a risky move. Your idea?

A: I'll tell you how that came about. I was in the marketing department, and my father wanted us to introduce pottery sooner than the marketing team was ready to do it. He wanted to introduce the whole product line in about six months.

• •

CDs in the Changer

Motown by Michael McDonald

Shaman by Carlos Santana

The Very Best of Fleetwood Mac by Fleetwood Mac

Classic Yo-Yo by Yo-Yo Ma

Hotel California by The Eagles

• •

I used to spend Sunday afternoons with a bucket of fried chicken at his house, and the conversation naturally went to what was going on in the business. A couple of weeks before our convention, he said, "We really need to introduce the pottery line sooner." But I said we just couldn't get it done. We hadn't even talked to a manufacturer yet. It was just the idea my father had. My job, in the 16 years I worked with him at the basket company after college, was figuring out how to put his ideas into action, figuring out how to get it done.

Of course, my timeline was a bit too long for him, "Give us 12 months to get it done."

He was, "No, get it done sooner."

I thought that we had agreed we would disagree, so I thought I had won. But he goes to our convention and announces to our national sales force that we were going to have the line launched in six months—to three or four thousand people! I'm backstage in shock. I can't believe he's doing that. But it gave us the incentive. It gave us the momentum, and we got it done. Central Ohio is known for pottery, and Zanesville is known as "Clay City."

. . . .

BOOKS ON THE NIGHTSTAND

Seeking Firm Footing: America in the World in the New Century by **Ambassador Richard S. Williamson (U.S. Representative to the United Nations Commission on Human Rights)**

Michelangelo and the Pope's Ceiling by **Ross King**

Longaberger: An American Success Story by **Dave Longaberger**

. . . .

My grandfather J.W. Longaberger made pottery baskets for all the local family-owned pottery companies. That's how we got into the basket craft. It was before conveyor belts. He made very sturdy baskets with metal strips that were used to haul the green-ware **[pottery before it has been fired]**. They'd slide the baskets over the floor. So we knew who could make the pottery. We came up with a few designs of mixing bowls, and the only concession I got from Dad was when he wanted five colors and I gave him four.

Q: Hah, that's not bending very much, that's not much of a concession at all.

A: And an extra month for the introduction. That's what I got. But he was right. He was exactly right. And that business is probably $175 million a year for us right now. What it showed me was that many of the things I learned in college, what works in a classroom to get you an "A," works a little differently and at a different pace in the real world. The appeal of our products is simple—people enjoy them. Our baskets tend to bring people some affordable luxuries [at] a difficult time and are something they can use every day. They're functional and will last a lifetime.

Q: Is the Internet a blessing or a curse for your sales model of independent consultants?

A: A blessing, an absolute blessing. We do not sell directly to consumers on the Internet today. We leverage the Internet to communicate with our sales force and they are sending their orders in today directly on the Web. Otherwise, everyone had to hand-write the orders. If you mail them in from California, it took eight days to get here. Now our associates can push a button, the order is entered and it's ready to go. Our commitment is to our sales force. We just invested $50 million into an enterprise resource system—a software package where everything works together.

Our company started with one computer in 1984. We patch-worked everything on top of that PC system and one day we realized that the volumes we were doing, where we wanted to go in the future—such as giving our customers direct shipment and giving our sales associates an ability to work with us quickly—meant that we needed to make some big changes. So we moved to a new system and every single process of our business has been changed.

We're celebrating our 30th anniversary this year. I've been working here 20 years in January. Every so many years or when you hit certain volumes, you've got to rebuild yourself; you've got to reinvent yourself. The economy can give you the incentive to look and see how you can do things better.

Q: Your baskets have been fixed in the Heritage of America, the country-style of decorating, yet many of your products should appeal to people on the Gold Coast of Chicago or Manhattan; very, very sleek—great contemporary lines and qualities.

A: Yes, exactly. It's not only people in the suburbs or rural areas who appreciate owning a piece of American craftsmanship. Our baskets are truly a piece of Americana that is difficult to find these days. That is our mission, to bring our products to everybody who wants to own a slice of America.

Q: Many companies probably want to link sales people back to production and production to sales people, and bring marketing into the loop. How do you bring down the walls and the resentment?

A: At our company, it's a wonderful thing. We have a connection between departments. Families stick together, and that's what we have here, a family. I think my father deserves credit for that—his speed as a leader. He didn't talk to people in solos. To him it was always, "We're all in this together."

We've always had tours of our manufacturing facility, not by design but because people were always interested in the craft. They would just stop by. One of the things I did when I was home from college was give tours in the summer. We didn't have scheduled tours. People would come by the plant and say, "Can we take a tour?"

Dad or someone would call me and say, "Hey, we have a tour that wants to go through." People were fascinated by the plant. They were able to talk to employees. They'd ask, "Tell me how you make that basket."

Today, we have 600,000 people a year come through our plant. We have a make-a-basket program and a traveling make-a-basket program that goes out across the country to sales associates' meetings. It's about the craft.

Q: Did he foresee at the beginning a network of tens of thousands of sales associates? How did that happen?

A: In the very beginning, the mid-1970s, Dad saw a rejuvenation of an interest in crafts. He had a little restaurant at the end of town and people were driving through Dresden to go up to Roscoe Village, an old restored canal town and Dad thought, *What's going on up there?*

So he drove up and saw what it was: one of the workshops had a store that sold a bunch of turn-of-the-century crafts. And there were some baskets in there. My father, very proud of my family's heritage in basket making, said, "Hey, my father's baskets are nicer than these." So he came home and asked my grandfather to make a few baskets and he, in turn, went back up there and sold them. He became our first sales associate.

The story is that we had a woman who used to come here to his little shop and she'd buy 10 baskets at a time. Big baskets. He asked, "Why are you doing that?" She said that she worked for another direct-selling company and sold kitchenware. She used the baskets to carry the kitchenware to home shows and that when she got to the home shows, people would ask, "Where'd you get the basket?" She'd tell the story about this little town and how the basket was made, and that's when Dad said, "Hey, that's a way to sell—tell the story."

So he started holding home shows in this area. He would talk about how the basket was made, his family history, about the eleven brothers and sisters in the Depression who helped make baskets when they could, how it was a well-made basket that would last a lifetime. He acknowledged that the baskets were not cheap, but that they were made with American labor and how the artisans earned every dime.

FAVORITE MEAL

"Chicken, mashed potatoes, corn and my mother's homemade noodles."

One thing led to another. We got to 70,000 associates through word-of-mouth. It probably wasn't until 1992 that we consistently started making money, but that's one of the benefits of being privately owned. My father always believed that if you made a little bit of money, you poured it back into the business. We still do that today, it's just that there's a lot more zeros behind the number. Our six largest states are Ohio, Illinois, Indiana, Pennsylvania, Virginia and California. About four years ago, I invested in a design team and a design center. We have an incredible group of artists who work in new concepts.

You know, I don't think people change. People still value Americana, time-honored crafts. We have 65 year-old collectors and we have 22 year-old collectors. Tastes may change but attention to design—that always stays in style.

6

✳Persistence

Kenneth S. Lowe, *E.W. Scripps*

In 1992, a forty-something, mid-level television executive came before the board of directors of the E.W. Scripps Co. in Cincinnati with a magazine display rack, a bunch of glossy magazines about the home, and a mission: convince the board of this stodgy newspaper company to create a cable television division.

The dream? To invest millions of dollars in an all–digital television production facility and satellite feed in Knoxville to create cable networks for North American homeowners, hand–crafters, and do-it-yourself fans.

Kenneth Lowe was that rising executive within the Scripps broadcast television division, a former disc jockey from

Southern Broadcasting, who came to Scripps in 1980 to become general manager of the company's radio properties.

With the magazine stand as a backdrop, Lowe told the board that a tremendous advertising opportunity existed for any company that could create the same product but do it for television viewers instead of magazine subscribers. It was a niche that no other broadcaster had mined.

The board gave him the go-ahead, and money poured into the venture. By 1996, four years later, the company had spent $26 million on its home-craft networks, with no black ink in sight. It would not be until 1998—after $49 million in losses —that the division found profits of $6 million. The momentum continued to build and in the decade after that meeting with directors, Lowe's idea for a cable network covering home and garden produced revenues of $2 billion for the company and profits of $465 million. It was a grand slam in the bottom of the ninth with two outs and trailing by three runs. But Lowe, now 53, never doubted the appeal of the category.

Question: These offerings of The Food Network and HGTV—and other cable offerings from the E.W. Scripps Co. —what is so appealing to Mr. and Mrs. Average? Why are these shows so popular with so many people?

Answer: It's interesting, the word we got back almost from day one with Home and Garden and The Food Network is that it's addictive. People tell us they leave it on all the time.

I don't think there's one particular reason but a combination. One was our timing. We were moving [away] from the "Me Generation" of the 1980s. As those folks were going out to start families and buy homes, they went from "I Want My MTV" to "I Want My HGTV." It was relevant to their lives and where they were—that pig in the python called the Baby Boomers.

That paralleled the growth curve of the Home Depots and the Lowe's Home Improvement Warehouses really taking off. It also coincided with women becoming more involved than ever with home repair and home remodeling. As a matter of fact, Home Depot started a bridal registry so women could come in and register for power tools. It was relevant programming.

And then, believe it or not, another piece of it was that these became alternative, or almost default, channels. They didn't have sex. They didn't have violence and they didn't have car crashes. They didn't have loud noises. They presented useful information in an entertaining way. I think they stood out because of that. As people were plowing around the channels they came upon us and thought, "Well, here's a channel. Things look nice. People are talking to me, appreciating my sensitivity." So they thought that this would be their channel, they thought, "Somebody has created this for me."

We got a lot of feedback early on from people who thanked us for a channel they didn't have to worry about when their child walked into the room.

Q: When you kick-started this, you got lots of emails. The president of one of your networks told me—and I believe him—that he read every one of them. Did you read them, too, for the feedback?

A: Quite a bit. One of the things I insisted upon from day one, because Scripps was putting this together, that the programming had to have credibility. By that I mean, because it was from Scripps coming from newspapers, what we did on television had to be above reproach. Not only because of Scripp's long–standing content initiatives from an ethics basis but, quite frankly, viewers are so smart today that if you put programming on that is in any way not clean and clear or if you blur the line between editorial and advertorial, they smell it. So we wouldn't do product placement. Nor would we allow sponsors to come in and use their advertising dollars as leverage to get us to use their products in programming.

We knew there would be a lot of questions about this programming, so, from the beginning, we set up a call center. At the time when we launched, it was the only cable network that had a call center. The idea was to make an immediate connection with the viewer, so viewers could get feedback and information right away as they were watching. We'd get calls like, "Gee, I'm really interested in that couch," or "I'm really interested in a particular faucet."

We had a referral list. We didn't mind giving them the

information or helping them find the information. People couldn't believe we weren't charging for that information.

It was true customer service and really, as you look ahead, that's where businesses are going to rise and fall in the future. It's all about customer service, the relationship to the customer. And it doesn't matter if it's a restaurant or retail or what your company is. We were doing this in 1994—selfishly—because we wanted to grow the network and be in contact with the viewer from day one.

For the first few months, I read the emails and letters. I literally tried to answer each one but soon it got out of hand. We were overwhelmed. The number we get now is in the thousands per week. But people remember that, they remember how we talked to them and how we listened to them. These are not overly complex things.

• •

CDs in the Changer

On the Moon by Peter Cincotti

Genius Loves Company by Ray Charles

License to Chill by Jimmy Buffett

• •

Early on, I would try to call some cable networks to ask about their programming because I wanted information, and I would be told, "There's no department for that sir, sorry."

I was shocked. It was like, "You've got to be kidding me," especially on the information-based stuff. Now a lot of it has shifted over onto the Internet because people can interact. In the early days of the Food Network, people had to send a self-addressed stamped envelope. Now the Internet has really helped us. I like to say we were interactive before interactive was cool. *We answered our phones!* That's interactivity.

Q: Your radio news background probably led you to the notion that when a phone rings, you pick it up. Is that at the root of Scripps Network's approach; customer service—do not fear interaction?

A: Yes, and always, always be straightforward. If you don't have the answer, tell them. If you can't find the answer, tell them. If you can get the answer, tell them. In many cases we'd say we don't have that so we'll get back to you.

A lot of what we executed with HGTV is the guerilla marketing that comes from radio. Radio, really, to me is the first one-to-one media, and cable is becoming more like radio in these targeted channels. You turn on Home and Garden Television all day and what do you get? Home and garden television. You might not be into landscaping. You might not be into interior design. But you're in the genre.

• •

BOOKS ON THE NIGHTSTAND

Big Russ and Me: Father and Son: Lessons of Life by Tim Russert

The Probability of God by Steven D. Unwin

The 21 Irrefutable Laws of Leadership by John C. Maxwell

and Zig Ziglar

• •

If you turn on a jazz station, if you turn on a country station, you know what you get and you tend to leave it on. That's the way cable is evolving. Oddly enough, you have a lot of ex-radio people in cable. Bob Pittman, Lee Masters, on and on. It's targeted. It's information-based and it fits with a lot of the Scripps mantra on the content side: *Information that's useful.*

If you go back to old man E. W. Scripps, the symbol of this company is a lighthouse. Give people light and they will find their way. It's interesting that 120-some years later, it still rings true, whether it's the Internet, whether it's a newspaper, whether it's a television station. We merely gave people what we thought they wanted, and fortunately we were right.

Q: Is there a risk to dilution of a core audience? HGTV gives birth to *Food*. *Food* gives birth to *Fine Living* and *DIY* (Do–It–Yourself). Are you cannibalizing, Balkanizing a core audience?

A: Candidly, yes. Because if we don't, somebody else will. If you go back and look at Scripps in the early 1990s, when I first brought the cable network plan to Larry Leser and Bill Burleigh, they looked at it and said, "This probably will be part of the cable network trend that takes viewers away from our broadcast television stations. It takes dollars away and viewing will go down."

We said, "Yes."

And they said, "Well, the best defense is a good offense." I think you have to attack yourself smartly and know that you know best of all where there are opportunities. We view this strictly as opportunistic and not necessarily attacking our core brands, but launching flanker businesses.

To give you an example: one of the challenges of *Home and Garden*, really—and it was something I was concerned about—was how to create a channel for people interested in home repair and remodeling *and* gardening *and* landscaping *and* interior design *and* decorating? That's not necessarily one viewer. However, we were able to do it by tying it all together with a feeling that you might not necessarily be into gardening but if you watch you might learn something. Whatever the subject, we try to make it interesting. And that's what we get back. People say they're not interested in decorating, but they love the show, *"Designing for the Sexes,"* because they can relate to it. That particular element allowed me to put together a network that's actually five networks in one. As we go forward, there will be more fragmentation.

For example, the TiVos, the replays, the personalized viewing—people are going home and dialing up exactly what they want to watch, when they want to watch it. At 8:17, not nine o'clock or 10 o'clock. HGTV becomes the big brand but there's also a gardening channel and home remodeling and improvement channel. That may be all you're interested in but you go to the mother brand. Fragmentation doesn't scare us.

There's a great marketing book called *Differentiate or Die: Survival in our Era of Killer Competition* by Jack Trout and Steve Rivkin. It has a chapter: "Here's the 1970s, Here's the 1990s." There was one brand of contact lens maker in the 1970s, there's 360 now; 74 vehicle styles then, 500 plus now. It just gives you an indication that proliferation and fragmentation is not going to stop.

People like choices. People like over-choices. It gets harder and harder to launch new products, but consumers demand that the new products be on the shelves.

Q: You are probably not a guy who's content to sit on three or four brands. What do you spin out next? A business channel? A recreational sport channel?

A: Home Depot and Lowe's Home Improvement Warehouse have stated that within the next five years 30 percent of the business at their stores will be to professionals. We are waiting for the technology; but a business-to-business site, a Home and Garden Professional, which targets contractors, plumbers, landscapers, people in the business side, is a strong prospect.

A lot of that is informational, long-distance learning trends, in part, tied to technology and the roll out of digital set top boxes and video-on-demand. These delivery systems are not that far away. To serve new channels we have a production facility in place that cranks out programming very efficiently, allowing us to move into other areas very easily.

It's not as easy for others to do the cost-effective programming that we can do. We're non-union. We have our own music publishing company, our own graphics. We have 35 mm film that we shoot in Knoxville. We also have a smaller version of a production company in Los Angeles, and we do quite a bit of shooting in New York for *Food*. We're agile. I wouldn't rule anything out at this point. It's going to be targeted content and we think we're set up nicely.

Q: Burton Jablin [President of HGTV], told me he had an inkling of the imminent success of the network when he was at a booth at the Knoxville *Home and Garden* show in 1994. He showed up with a camera crew, hoping to find some people who knew what the network was about, and that instead of finding a few people stopping by, there were lines all day long. Do you remember that booth? What was your moment when you realized, "We have something BIG here?"

A: I sure do remember that booth. For me it was the day we launched: December 30. We were all physically and mentally exhausted because we pushed to this launch day. We launched at 7 a.m. and by about 10 a.m., 11 a.m., our phone started ringing.

These were the Christmas holidays, remember, and the sales manager of one of our advertisers called me. He was so excited he could barely speak. He said he went into his office over the weekend, and their 1-800 telephone was blown out of the wall. He said, "You guys don't understand. The only place we're advertising is on HGTV!" Well, this was the first day we'd launched. There was no promotion or publicity and people, I guess, were finding the channel by dialing around on the cable system. And he says that nothing had ever, ever happened like this. His company had been advertising for 50 years. He said that we were really on to something.

And as we were sitting there having that conversation, my assistant walks in and says the switchboard downstairs is lit up like a Christmas tree. People are calling and saying, "I love this channel," and "Where have you guys been?"

• •

FAVORITE MEAL

"Anything my mother makes but if I had to pick one: corn bread, pinto beans, collard greens and country ham."

• •

What's even more ironic is we didn't have a telephone number listed. On-screen we had a credit about Knoxville, Tenn. So some operators there were aware of the network and were telling people to call this Cinatel Production number. It was instantaneous and almost surreal. The first thing I said was, "My college roommate [Gary Dees, Los Angeles entertainer and radio personality] is playing a joke on me with four or five of his buddies." As we went through the day it began to sink in a little bit.

I said, "Look, let's get some promos cut at the convention center. Strong-arm some people and put them in front of the camera." But we didn't have to do that. It was like we were giving folks a script.

It's like anything. You plan, you work, you research, but until the curtain goes up, you don't know if the play is going to fly or not. You think it will. You have a pretty good feeling, but it's up to the audience. I think that our wildest expectations were truly met and exceeded. From there, the ball just started rolling.

Q: Last time I looked, Scripps Networks' revenues are moving at a 23 percent annual growth rate. Where will they be in a few years from now?

A: It is the growth engine of the company, and when you have mature properties, like newspapers and television stations, there is no way they're going to grow at these kinds of rates. It's a little hard to speculate, and *Home and Garden* will slow down a little bit, but there are a few categories of advertisers that we've never tapped into. Some are obvious, say, fast foods, which usually only advertise with younger demographics. We might tap into that.

But categories of advertising at Scripps Networks are pretty much ubiquitous. When we broke through 30 million households, we got into automotive and financial services. There are very few advertising segments that we don't hit. Fast food and beer, which are typically heavy male sports—that's not one we ever expected to get, but we did.

The good news is the feedback we get from advertisers: the ringing of the cash register. There is now an ability to bookmark efficiency of advertising.

Your analogy of cable networks to radio is pretty good. Our audiences are targeted; we know the psychographics and demographics, and in the case of *Home and Garden* and *Food* networks, our viewers are consistently in the top five in household incomes. These networks reach very, very strong demographics. That bodes well for high advertising rates and future growth. I won't put a number on what that growth will be. But you must absolutely protect your brand and what it means to people. If you let it drift a little, then you lose so much. It's the old General Patton line: "I don't like to regain ground that we've already taken."

Q: The studio and systems in Knoxville are all digital and extremely expensive. It's brought you a digital library of tens of thousands of hours of content that is, essentially, already paid for. Talk about the decision to go digital.

A: Digital and set-top boxes are the future. So if you're not creating content that works for that, if it's just going to continue to be linear type programming that can't be broken apart, then you've got a little bit bigger of a challenge than what we'll face.

That's why *DIY* [Do–It–Yourself Network] is the next phase of converging video and the Internet. It's an exciting time, and we've got a great facility and great people on board. We've brought people in from New York to Knoxville and you can tell, they're going, "Ugh, Knoxville."

Then we give them a tour of the facilities. They get a look at the future and they walk out of there with their tongues hanging out.

7

☀Turnaround

Marvin Lewis, *Head Coach, Cincinnati Bengals*

At some point many companies find that revenues have
swooned, profits have drifted away on the wind and investors
are ready to float the life-boats. When that happens, it's time
for a turnaround consultant. Few men have had as audacious a
turn-around challenge as Marvin Lewis, the head coach of the
Cincinnati Bengals.

While a page or two would not be long enough to describe
the trauma that the Bengals inflicted on local fans in the 1990s,
one word can sum up the team before the arrival of Lewis:
abysmal. The 2002 team posted the worst record in franchise
history at 2-12. In more than a decade after their last play-off
appearance in 1990, the Bengals racked up a miserable 55-137

record. And then came Lewis, a demanding professional who had studied under San Francisco 49-er legend Bill Walsh. Lewis, who set an NFL record for Fewest-Points-Scored-Against-a-Team-in-a-Season, while he was defensive coordinator for the Baltimore Ravens, was a fly-on-the wall when he arrived in Cincinnati as head coach.

Nobody was immune to his scrutiny and after learning what he needed to know, he began to act, to shake up attitudes. He railed at those who left used ankle tape on the floor for somebody else to pick up. Lewis offered up symbols like extension cords in every locker to imply it was time to extend the season. He reached out to luxury suite owners—calling each and every one. He promised that success awaited this team, and he would see to it that competitive football would return to Cincinnati.

In his first two seasons as a head coach, Lewis and the Bengals managed a 16-16 record. True to his nature, Lewis was far from satisfied. People pay to see winners.

Question: It's 1980, Reno McKee Stadium, and the college team is down by a few points. You're a senior linebacker and you think you can make something happen. So you slice through, block a punt, turn the game around and right there, remembers your former coach two decades later. That play turns the season around and the next season, too. You did no chest thumping. Remember the play?

Answer: No, no chest pumping. Yeah, I remember it. We were playing Nevada Reno, who had a better football team, or at least had brighter stars. I remember it was late in the game and I felt like I could block the kick, and I told our coaches that. And they said, "Well, go block it." I did and one of our guys picked it up and ran it in for a touchdown. We eventually won the football game.

It was kind of the turnaround of the program there at Idaho State. The year previous, we had gone 0-11, and that year we ended up 6-5 and played the last game at Boise State for the conference championship. It was a great turnaround for the program. The next year, while I was coaching, we won the National 1AA Championship. So, in two years, we'd gone from

0-11 to a national championship and 12-1.

Q: Do people need to get a taste of losing to know they don't like it?

A: I think you do learn some lessons in losing—and you can learn some lessons in winning, too. But sure, you have to take something from losing. It makes you stand up and notice that you don't like it and that you have to find your way out of it. People who have substance to them, they find a way out. They figure out a way to get out of that plight.

Q: One notion about leadership is that sometimes people follow leaders because they're curious. They want to know, "Where's this wacky guy going?"

A: In sports and, I think, in any business, you're all united for the same thing. When you gather people with the same goal, the same philosophy, the same passion, and you cultivate the ones who are on the fence, it breeds more passion.

When you have people looking at the underside, the negative side of something, then you're going to have a difficult time winning them over and you're probably better off changing those people out and getting some new people.

• •

CDs in the Changer

The Isley Brothers Greatest Hits Vol. 1 **by The Isley Brothers**
Soundtrack from Bad Boys II **by Various Artists**

• •

There are always going to be people who are—I want to say—"cautious." They're second-guessers, the naysayers; they probably live their whole life that way, and they've never had a chance to experience being as good as they could have been because they were never cut loose. They never buy in totally. They never think, *Let's just follow this guy and do this and let me do my part.* They never ask, *"Can the whole be greater than the sum of its parts."* They never ask, *"Can I take my role and just run with it?"*

Q: Do you think of yourself as a leader?

A: I have to be a leader. That's what the position is. I think that, throughout my life, I've somewhat put myself in that role because I want to win. So every time you do something, if you're going to spend the time at it, you might as well be good at it.

I've not been a person who's unhappy to follow, but if everybody just sits there, then I'm going to take control of a situation and get out of this. I was a leader on the college team, in high school, in youth football, and in everything I'd ever done on a football field.

I wasn't always the guy organizing this or that. Sometimes you're just a part of it. But when they pass the torch, you've got to be a leader. We all have a role and responsibilities, but when your time comes, you've got to be prepared.

Q: As a leader, what's the most annoying thing you deal with day in and day out?

A: I think jealousy. A lot of people get hung up on what someone is going to say or think about them, and so they spend all their time worried about that, instead of focusing their energy on just doing. They stall themselves from being very good at something because they're worried about the perception.

Q: Do you need eye-to-eye contact with somebody you're thinking of bringing onto a team?

A: Somewhat. But I think their day-to-day actions confirm. People get three chances. You can sit here in this room, and I can have a guy nod his head and tell me, "Yeah, I'm going to go do that." Alright, that's chance number one, although really chance number one is already done because chance number two is when we are in this room talking about it. Chance number three is when he doesn't do it again. Now we're through.

There's just not enough time. When you get into coaching, you realize that you don't get a chance to do it over again. There are no do-overs on Sunday. You have to get to a point where the guys on the team realize how important each and every practice play is, how important each and every individual rep is. That's a big change in atmosphere that leads to winning. There are no do-overs. When you don't get it right, you lose. We don't get a chance very often to go back and fix something, go back and mend it because it's already cost you something.

Hopefully, you learn a valuable lesson, but I think it's too hard to be successful in the NFL—or in any business—if you're always putting good money after bad. And that's what do-overs are about. It's all those sayings that come to mind, *"my mistake,"* for instance. Well, all that is, is people allowing mediocrity to happen. When I hear *"Let me be honest with you"*—well, right there, up goes the red flag. Most times the guy is lying to me. I think in this business, our shelf life, our window of opportunity is too short and you have to focus the guys on that. There's not an opportunity to get many chances back. If you don't do it right the first time, you don't really have time to do it again.

Q: Hate to Monday-morning-Quarterback you here, but when you're down by a touchdown or two, your starting quarterback has been sacked six times, why not put in Mr. Heisman, your million-dollar back-up QB over there on the bench? Play a little playground football? "Go long, Chad?" Two or three plays, and you're back in the game, maybe in the play-offs?

A: You don't want to get him killed. That's not the best chance for a guy to get in there and play. It's a bad atmosphere because the guys on the other side are going to show him. There's no reason to subject him to that. Also, it's a confidence thing. You are bringing in instability into the position.

Q: Joe Torre of the Yankees, he could care less what his starter thinks when he pulls him. Why not a short-relief quarterback, like the short-relievers in baseball?

A: Baseball is different. Baseball is an individual sport. Well, Michael Vick started that way as a rookie. First, they played him at home for a couple of series, then they played him a little longer, but by the end of the rookie year, they were only playing him on first and second downs because he was struggling on third down. Those things happen. But I've got to do what I feel best about, and I don't think at that point it's a good time for us to put a quarterback in jeopardy. You start a media circus about your starting quarterback. There is indecision. It's not fair when you have just one game to win to go to the play-offs.

Q: Talk about decisive action.

A: You have to have a sense of direction and when your direction isn't right, you've got to fix it. You need to analyze the entire situation of what is best to win a game. In the 2003-2004 season, every game but two came down to the last possession. That's another part of it.

Q: At the end of each season, you give every player a sheet of paper with key dates on it and your expectations, boom, boom, boom, right down the line. Why do you do that? Clear expectations and communications?

A: I saw back in 1986 or 1987, when I was part of the San Francisco 49ers organization under Coach Walsh, the thing that struck you was that everything was detailed and planned-out in advance.

• •
BOOKS ON THE NIGHTSTAND

The Big O: My Life, My Times, My Game: The Biography of
Oscar Robertson **by Oscar Robertson**

• •

These guys have families. These guys have kids. They have responsibilities, and they need to know what's coming up next, whether it's during the season, or after the season. You don't want their wife worried about when they're going to go shopping, when they're going to have a baby. When are we going to do this? When are we going to do that? I think it makes everybody—the player's wives, the coaches' wives, my wife—I think it makes everybody more in tune that this is the next time we meet up again. This is when mini-camp starts. This is when our off-season starts.

I think when you get towards the end of the season, it's important to give a guy a goal, "This is what I feel you need to get better at, for you to become a better player." That's all our job is: make these guys the best player they can be. That's it.

In turn, that makes us the best team and that's why people will want to play for you. They have trust that you are going to make them the best football player that they can be.

What we've been selling is that we want a player to come here because we can take him to this higher level. And that, in turn, takes us to that level as a team, and if that happens, we all reach our goal, which is to win a championship.

Q: Back to that 0-11 season in Boise. I realized, after talking to the trainer, that you guys got a new weight room out of it and then I started thinking, "Wait, Marvin Lewis comes to the Bengals when the Bengals were sucking wind and the first thing he does is get a new weight room, just like back at Idaho State."

A: Players talk. They knew what the perception was in Cincinnati. I knew what the perception was. I came twice in the interview process. I came back a second time to come here. To me it was important to see what I was representing. There are 32 head coaching jobs in the NFL, and for me, it was going to be a great opportunity—no matter what. There would be practice fields, there would be 53 players, and I would be paid more than I'd ever been paid before, so that didn't matter. What was important to me was, *What did we have to offer to coaches, their families, players and their families?* That's why I wanted to come here.

· ·
FAVORITE MEAL ON THE ROAD
Mexican
· ·

First thing I see is the stone on the floor of the elevator, the wood trim inside the elevator. We go upstairs, and I don't know if I actually looked in here (his stark office), but I remember seeing the coasters with the Bengal logo in all the conference rooms upstairs. I remember seeing the logo on all the chairs. Well, this was not the perception of what people had given me about the Cincinnati Bengals. There was a lot of time, money and intricate thinking going into building this place.

Then you walked down into the locker room and it hit

me: *There are no stools for the players!* That's their living space. We had a beautiful lounge but it wasn't being taken care of at all. We are going to refurbish that. We've changed out the video games to offer something the players want to do. There are computer terminals now.

• •

ON THE COFFEE TABLE

Jet and *Sports Illustrated*

• •

We want this to be a place where the players will want to spend their time. You have a bad football team when the guys can't wait to get out of here at the end of the day. That's the atmosphere that has changed. A work space is actually living space. It had to be done.

Q: Something as simple as a stool resonates with players, resonates with people. Somebody comes to you and says, "I want to help you with your career." Well, you have to give him the benefit of the doubt and you will...

A: Work harder. You have to grow your organization from the ground up. You have to empower people. If you're aiding and helping the 53rd player or the person who cleans up after the players in the locker room, or the person serving our food — if their standard has risen, it's easier to raise the standards of others, too. That's important. Here's another example:

We want guys to hydrate. We want guys to drink Gatorade and water. Well, there were no dispensers other than little cups. So we went back to the refrigerator in the locker room so a guy could get Gatorade, water, and fruit after he's finished working out.

We want them drinking. We had six, seven guys a game taking IV's at half-time. Well, there's a lot more to that. You're trying to get them to hydrate during the week, during practice. You can't hydrate on the plane en route to a game. You don't begin to eat right just because the season starts. It's got to be a daily thing, year-round. That's what we had to convince guys about. It led to us being healthier, stronger all year around.

We have meals downstairs with chefs who want to see our guys succeed. They're not just doing the job. They're doing the job with love. At first the guys didn't think the food was that good, and it took me coming in from outside to say that we have a great thing going with the food. We had to tailor the meals so we don't have a heavy lunch meal and then go out and practice an hour an a half later when everybody wants to go take a nap. After we win, we have an omelet bar every Wednesday and Thursday. Those are the little rewards. When it's cold on Wednesday and Thursday, we come in and have hot soup or a broth.

It's the little things that our guys appreciate; the little details say we care. That creates commitment and a winning attitude in the players and the entire organization.

8

❈Finding Channels

Dr. Karen Stephenson, *CIA Analyst*

Karen A. Stephenson, Ph.D., is a crime-fighter who works in terrorism prevention, and with corporate clients to identify the potential for corporate fraud before it happens.

A pioneer in the emerging field of Social Network Analysis, Stephenson believes that astute leaders who want to refine an organization must identify key people before making any significant change. For executives to know what is happening within their companies, they must be aware of the informal hierarchies that exist outside the traditional pyramids of power. In other words, some people have more ability to motivate co-workers—or de-motivate them—than their titles or roles would imply.

Stephenson has a varied academic background: a

Ph.D. in Anthropology from Harvard University, an M.A. in Anthropology from the University of Utah, and a B.A. in Art and Chemistry from Austin College.

A corporate anthropologist, she is professor of management at Harvard University and has been an advisor to the CIA, Hughes Aircraft, AOL Time-Warner, IBM and TRW Inc. Stephenson is the chief executive of NetForm International Inc., and speaks on the scientific principles of network management at California State University, Columbia, MIT, and University of California (Berkeley and Los Angeles).

• •

CDs in the Changer

Spain: The collection from Cafe del Mar
Compiled by Jose Padilla (her favorite artist)

Out of Zuell **by AR Rahman**

All My Favourite Things **by A Man Called Adam**

• •

Question: If the people who are the chatty ones—the gatekeepers, hubs and pulse takers—get laid off, won't other hubs, gatekeepers and pulse takers take their place and the organization will sail on renewed and reinvigorated?

Answer: Yes, there is natural knowledge progression, but if all your top-tier people leave at once, the top five percent, it is too much of a shock to the networks. Because it is a shock to the networks, it can sometimes destroy a culture. When people in the government are asking me to find and destroy terrorist networks, that's what we do. We try to find the top five percent and take them out at once because that will be effective. In an organization, one person or a couple of people can leave, but five percent cannot leave at once. It will be too difficult for the network to recover.

Q: Have you worked internationally on the terrorist network problem or is your focus domestic?

A: It's international. These terrorist networks are everywhere. You have to be able to see the structure of these networks, and if you can't see it then you have to come up with methods to deduce the structure.

The process is similar to what we do in organizations, but in the corporate world we do it for positive and proactive reasons. Even when we deduce network structures to find or anticipate fraud, we are trying to protect the people before they commit the fraud. These individuals are usually very smart and very innovative, and we want them to stay with the organization instead of going to jail. We try to find folks who are creatively manipulating and finessing the system and point them in the right direction. This methodology is restorative in nature and regenerative.

Q: Does the methodology evolve? Is it synergistic? Does it evolve and change as you move through the deductive process?

A: The methodology has evolved over a 30-year period. The basic scientific principles of network structures remain the same. The methodology has improved because computers have improved. Visualization techniques have dramatically changed, and the Internet and access to the information has changed.

As business becomes increasingly aware that its culture is run by networks, rather than a hierarchy, a growing self-awareness has led to more sophisticated questions that hone in on specific applications: mergers and acquisitions, forms of restructuring. Strategically, how to design a better office and workplace environment; how to tell your consumer what and where to buy; how to pay for performance strategically; how to design a better office and workplace environment.

Q: Information is gathered through interviews with employees?

A: In the early days, yes. Now, because we're scanning for dimensions of knowledge, it becomes like an MRI. It's x-ray slices of an organization or social body. It's taking slices of knowledge, innovation, expertise, decision-making, issues like that. All of those slices, when taken together, make up the body of an organization. You ask a series of questions targeted at those dimensions, and those are really the networks of that dimension. You ask maybe seven to ten questions. We have 15 that really cover everything, but we never ask that many questions because we don't want to tire people out. We ask how people work with various dimensions of knowledge.

BOOKS ON THE NIGHTSTAND

Quantum Physics by John R. Gribbon

Quantum Reality: Beyond the New Physics by Nick Herbert

The Elegant Universe: Superstrings, Hidden Dimensions and the Quest for the Ultimate Theory by Brian Greene

MOST FREQUENTLY USED BOOK
Webster's Unabridged or the *Oxford English Dictionary*

There is nothing proprietary about the data collection methodology except that we are probably ahead of the market from the sophisticated tools we use. The optimization and measurement of these organizational networks are very proprietary. We've honed that over 30 years and constantly test against a database of over 300 examples.

Q: You're trained as an anthropologist and have lived as a cultural explorer in distant places: the Sahara, the jungles of Latin America, in life-threatening situations. Do you have any broad-brush conclusions about the American workplace and parallels to tribes?

A: I'm trained as a scientist, in chemistry, in physics and mathematics. I have undergraduate degrees in chemistry and art. I have a Master's in the mathematical modeling of human groups.

The workplace is going to be the icon for the new millennium in the way people think about culture and how they get along. The workplace is changing in place and space. It's virtual.

I've gone off and spent many years in the jungles of the Yucatan, and the Sahara in Egypt, doing unauthorized classical research. I just went out and did it and became good at it. People like *National Geographic* would pay me to find hidden treasure. That work prepared me for this kind of organizational work. I find what goes on inside of organizations is remarkably similar to what goes on in non-industrial tribal societies.

Basically, people are calculating. They're trying to figure out their relations to one another, whether that's biology or fictional relationships like organizational charts. People in head-hunting societies didn't have much violence at all, even though they were head-hunters. We're far more violent in some ways in our corporations. We physically don't go out and kill people but neither did tribal people. They did it ritualistically, and we do it ritualistically as well. We hunt heads. We take people down professionally. The behavior is the same, even behind the scenes.

• •

FAVORITE MEAL

Moroccan

• •

I don't think productivity and performance are lifesavers, either. If you are very good at what you do, sometimes you are targeted by those who would be jealous. I want to believe that the workplace can be a meritocracy. You know what they say—a cynic is a frustrated idealist. Even though I speak somewhat cynically about these realities, I fundamentally am an idealist and believe that you can create meritocracies and pay people for performance and have them aligned around objectives and goals.

Q: Flow in the workplace seems to be a pretty fleeting and capricious thing.

A: It is. But when you have flow, you look back on it and know you have it. I keep my eye on the prize and the prize is always the idea. You can heed—but don't concede—to politics. Keep your eye on the idea because there is authenticity around an idea, and people can never mistake your devotion and service to an idea as having anything to do with a personal agenda.

9

☀️Out-of-the-Box

Jeff "Skunk" Baxter, *Guitar Wizard*

For more than three decades, Jeff "Skunk" Baxter, 57, has been a pop and rock guitar wizard who has played with Steely Dan, Elton John, Dolly Parton, the Doobie Brothers and many others. Today, Baxter has a high-level Pentagon security clearance as a Department of Defense advisor to the Ballistic Missile Defense Organization and advises business leaders on tactics to encourage out-of-the-box strategies.

The journey from rock musician to defense analyst and business consultant may seem incongruous or even far-fetched, but Baxter's involvement stemmed from his strongly-held conservative views coupled with an interest in military history and hardware.

It was a fascinating metamorphosis. As gleaned

from a Doobie Brothers website, in the '80s, while his peers would drink beer and play video games on tour, Baxter buried himself in technical defense magazines. He found technology to be neutral, dependent upon the application. For instance, if TRW came up with new data compression algorithm for spy satellites, Baxter might see an application to a musical instrument or a hard disc recording unit. His interest in defense was born when one of Baxter's friends had to write an op-ed piece on NATO and weapons systems and asked Baxter to help. He was so inspired by the project, he wrote his own paper on missile defense and handed it to Congressman Dana Rohrbacher, who showed it to his associates.

"The next thing I knew," Baxter told one interviewer, "I was up to my teeth in national security, mostly in missile defense. Because the pointy end of the missile sometimes is not just nuclear, but chemical, biological or volumetric, I got involved in the terrorism side of things."

Question: Why do you have a perspective on out-of-the-box thinking and creativity? Why are you an expert?

Answer: I think it has to do with my transition from the area of music and entertainment as a guitarist to the arena of national security and more specifically in the area of ballistic missile defense. Being a guitarist is so vastly different from advising the folks on Capitol Hill on ballistic missile defense.

Q: What is it that you bring to the table that West Pointers otherwise can't see? Is it simply your perspective?

A: I think that is a lot of it. I have not been doctrinally trained in a certain area. My ability to analyze and look at situations from a different perspective isn't hampered by a certain type of thinking. I can see things from a different point of view. In war-gaming scenarios, I come to it from a red team perspective. Many times I've been successful simply because I don't apply what would be accepted thinking.

Q: The improvisational nature of music composition can that have an impact on Joe Bagadonuts, who has a hardware store in suburban Cincinnati? Should he be sitting down each week taking clarinet lessons to encourage creativity?

A: Well, that's not such a bad idea. One of the advantages to having a certain comfort level and ability in the music area means you have been able to use your left brain and right brain together in problem-solving. Improvisation is a combination of taking whatever it is you want to say musically and, right at the moment, drawing on your knowledge and ability, instantly creating a vocabulary stream to describe what you feel.

Many people don't learn to use the left-brain right-brain combination because they are brought up to think in a linear fashion. It is somewhat like learning to drive a car in a place where there is no rain and, then, how do you drive on a wet road? The question is, what do you know and how can you think on your feet to come up with a solution?

Q: Most people don't have the luxury of gazing each day at the Adriatic Sea or staring at the Julian Alps—getting lost in a beautiful landscape—as a way to encourage creativity. Is there something everybody can and should do every week to encourage creativity?

A: Most people have a hobby or something that they do that may or may not relate to the major area that they work in. Most people engage in that because they're looking to take a mental vacation to allow their batteries to recharge. That's extremely important.

It's the old idea of not being able to see the forest for the trees. If you don't get away from things, eventually you won't be able to get away from things at all. Music for a lot of people is a big part of that. By playing an instrument they practice a form of Zen. It allows you to get to a slightly different place. I recommend that highly—anything that temporarily takes your focus away from what it is you're trying to accomplish.

Q: Have you studied any great artists? Who is your favorite in any medium and what are the lessons for business?

A: I'm a huge fan of Ludwig van Beethoven. A lot of his

work has fairly simple chord changes. When I listen to much of his music, I think he used the simplicity of simple chord changes to make the music more accessible to people.

There is an old adage in music that you have simple chord changes with a complex melody or, the other way around, use complex chord changes with a simple melody. Beethoven was conscious about what the average person can assimilate and, on a lot of levels, he made his music accessible. That's a tenet I try to adhere to when I write music or when I play it.

It's a business lesson, as well. Make information accessible—something the average person can assimilate.

Q: Why should people listen to what you have to say?

A: Because I wanted to be involved in the national security arena and to do that, I've had to surmount certain obstacles. One obstacle was not having a background in national security. Another obstacle was coming to a place where people have a problem understanding how a musician, with no real understanding of the geo-strategic and geo-political situation, can evolve into an advisor to those with political and military responsibilities. I have a tremendous amount of passion about my country, its security, and democracy.

10

✵Steer the Ship

Louis V. Gerstner, Jr., *Former IBM Chairman*

Big Blue had a bad case of the blues when Louis V. Gerstner, Jr., was approached to turn around this American giant. Bleeding $8.1 billion, Gerstner, currently Chairman of the Carlyle Group, a holding company for a number of defense and energy companies, and former chief executive of RJR Nabisco and president of American Express, had a couple of choices when he became chief executive of IBM in March 1993. He could reinvent the high-tech titan, smash it into autonomous units, or even sell off IBM division by division.

Gerstner convinced the cadre of career IBMers that the company had to shift its focus. Personal computer turfwar already belonged to the more nimble Microsoft, Dell, Gateway, and a host of other providers. His big idea was to launch a technology services unit that focused on global sales, services, and the manufacture of semi-conductors and hard drives. By 2002, the reversal was complete. IBM had profits of $8 billion, and Gerstner was gone, the reins in the hands of Samuel Palmisano.

(From a Fifth Third Bancorp Seminar).

Question: What's the business climate in ten years?
Answer: In all my 40 years, I've never seen a more positive opportunity for business. I think we have one of the most extraordinary periods of economic growth before us that we'll ever see. I'm setting aside political issues, what politicians do, what happens with issues of security. But if you look at what's happening, you'll see that first of all, a marketplace that was closed for more than a half century, that represents a good third of the potential in the world has opened: China, India, Russia, Central Europe, the sub-continent beyond India. A huge market has opened that heretofore had been closed.

Secondly, information technology is in its infancy in its capacity for productivity, reach, and market-building activities. And thirdly, and this is probably least important, we have governments that are practicing, for the most part, a mercantile philosophy. In prior years, they were indifferent to it. That is no secret. So the next decade will be the most difficult competitively of any we have ever seen. It will be a white-knuckle decade of competition, and we will see a huge fall-out of winners and losers. An overcapacity exists in almost every industry in the world. Even the smallest company can exploit these new technologies and seek markets all over the world. We are going to see a real premium on leadership.

Q: When you were being recruited to IBM, how important was patriotism to you in deciding to take the job?
A: Well, they were getting pretty desperate. They couldn't find anybody willing to take the job. And I actually turned it down three times. They tried the Good Humor Man. They tried to get anybody they could find in the street. They came back to me the fourth time, and said they were going to call President

Clinton and have him call me.

Well, that had very little to do with it. One, I knew it was a bluff. Two, I knew the President wouldn't do it. And three, that wouldn't be a very good basis upon which to make a decision.

Q: Without a technology background, you took over the leading technology company in the world.

A: That was one of several reasons that I said I wasn't interested in the job. The board convinced me that it was not a technical issue, but a leadership issue. They turned out to be wrong. It really was a fundamentally technical challenge. I figured out that the people who developed software are a little bit like actuaries in the insurance industry. They really don't want you to understand what they're doing. You walk in and kind of get this picture of them brewing, that there are boiling cauldrons and that's how they do their work. The technology itself is difficult, but technologists like to make it even more difficult. The more difficult it is, the more needed they are.

Years ago I found a mentor who always kept a stack of work on his desk, but did nothing with it. I asked him about this one day and he told me, "Half the work will solve itself if you leave it alone." I've never forgotten that. And it's turned out to be true.

Q: Isn't changing the culture one of the challenges of a leadership role in a technology company?

A: I believe that one of the most important things a leader has to do in an organization is to continually drive responsiveness to change. The problem that IBM had was that it got so caught up with its own success that it started to focus inwardly. How can we duplicate this success, run training programs that tell us what we do all the time? How can we invent, look inwardly, and continue to replicate what we've done in the past? That's a good thing to do when you're successful: figure out what you're doing right and how to replicate it. The problem is that when the environment changes, you're still running the same engine inside, replicating things that have nothing to do with what's going on outside.

Successful companies constantly go through self-renewal. They are always driven by change and, therefore, their culture has to be one that accepts change, embraces change and therefore changes inside when outside conditions change. You have to have an ability to change when the market changes. At IBM there was something known as "push-back." Anybody in the company that didn't agree with something could push it back. But that was not very conducive to providing innovative solutions for the customer. When it started out it was a good idea, but it got corrupted.

• •

CDs in the Changer

Country Roads: Greatest Hits of John Denver **by John Denver**

The Best of the Three Tenors: Jose Carrerras, Placido Domingo and Luciano Pavarotti

La Boheme **by Puccini**

• •

Take the IBM dress code. In the 1930s, Thomas Watson Sr., the founder of the company, said to everybody that you should dress like the customer. Dark suits, white shirts, ties and wing-tips. That shows respect for the customer. Well, time goes by and all of a sudden our customers were not wearing wing-tips, white shirts and ties. Some were wearing that, and some were not. When I abolished the dress code, you would have thought I sold the company to the Russians. I didn't put another dress code in. I simply said, "Let's go back to old man Watson's premise of dress for the customer." Customers are coming in wearing black t-shirts, bell-bottoms and sandals, so you can wear those. But again, what we had was a corruption of something that made sense in the past but didn't make sense today.

I think brave leaders continually look at the company culture and ask one question: Are we doing the right thing? Are we valuing the right thing? Is the organization valuing the right thing? Or are we living off of a system that is out of date? It took probably three to four years before people really understood that we needed to change both the strategy and behavior at the company. Everybody thought all we'd do is change strategy or change prices or do an acquisition; that we'd do some *business* thing, and that would fix IBM.

Look at companies that got into this rigor mortis success syndrome, and all these CEOs who came in from the outside and failed. For the most part, they made acquisitions or brought in technology; but they never attacked the underlying problem, which is what do people do when they're on the mat. What do they value?

It took us probably three years to realize that we needed to change. We were into our fifth or sixth year before we really had the momentum of the change behind us. There were Bolsheviks hiding all over the company who wanted to go back to the old system of entitlement, presiding, and an internal hierarchy, as opposed to a hierarchy of customer first. It was hard for them to change.

Q: What are the biggest challenges that companies will face in the next decade?

A: The overcapacity that is growing around the world. The automobile industry has something like 15 to 20 million cars of excess capacity today and guess what? China is getting into the automobile business. China is going to add capacity. What do you do when you have overcapacity in the banking business, overcapacity in the insurance business? There's overcapacity in almost everything. And it's going to have to be solved over time.

There has been a lot of discussion about the out-sourcing of jobs in the United States and it is a fundamentally phony issue. We've been out-sourcing jobs in America for 150 years. We've been moving commodity-like, low-skill jobs offshore for years. The American consumer benefits enormously from low-price, high-quality products coming in as American workers gravitate up to higher skilled, higher quality jobs. They keep moving up the chain.

There's one problem. Our public school system is not producing skilled workers. We turn out 75,000 engineers. In India there are roughly 200,000. In China—400,000. They have figured it out. They've figured out that the key to economic growth is educated workers. We have a public school system that is a travesty and leaving behind millions of kids every year who simply cannot perform.

The issue is not out-sourcing of jobs. The issue is: Are we going to build the skills in our young people that will allow them to compete for jobs and compete on a global basis?

To me, if you're a business person you have two real issues. You've got to demand that public schools in America get fixed and that they deliver high-quality skills so that you can have a quality workforce because you are fighting for talent. The war for talent is going to get so progressively difficult because you are fighting for talent on both a macro and a micro level.

Q: How did you evaluate talent when you came to IBM? How did you energize the workforce there?

A: I got roundly criticized after about six months. People would ask, "What are you doing? How come you haven't fired anybody?"

Let me tell you something—you walk into a company that is bleeding to death and almost ready to go under, and it has a whole bunch of technology that you don't know anything about. What do you do? Fire everybody and bring in a bunch of people who are like you, who know nothing? I figured the system, the culture, was over-riding the talent that was within the company. So I started to articulate the values that were going to describe IBM: customer-specific, team-oriented, hard workers and not "presiders." We were going to be direct with each other rather than communicating through customer-speak or IBM-speak. I started exhibiting that behavior and making sure it happened immediately, and people began to get the message and began to perform.

We were losing a billion dollars, and I put a senior guy in charge and told him to bring me the full picture. I saw him three days later and asked him what he had learned. He said, "Oh, I'm going to call somebody." Three days later, I saw him, "What are you going to do?" He said, "I'll call Joe and find out." So I said, "Wait a minute, who is this Joe fellow? I'll call him." I'm not interested in people who preside.

The higher up in an organization you get, the harder

you work. I discovered there were people who were saying to their troops that they were sorry that the troops had to work Saturdays and Sundays, and then they themselves wouldn't go in. I said if you make your people work Saturdays and Sundays, then you're there, too. You're there when they show up, and you're there when they leave. Don't sit in your office on Monday morning and wait for their results. Well, the message started to get out.

We had a couple of public hangings of people whose behavior was different from what we wanted to do.

All of a sudden, people began to thrive and those were the people I picked for leadership positions at the company. I had to bring some people from outside—marketing and HR—and then 10,000 people started to figure it out. They started moving the ship.

· ·

BOOKS ON THE NIGHTSTAND

Alexander Hamilton **by Ron Chernow**

The Tiananmen Papers **by Public Affairs Books**

—*"A fascinating book about people who run China today and their thoughts and activities."*

The House Sitter **by Peter Lovesey**

· ·

We made everybody understand that they had to live up to certain values, particularly on teamwork. It wasn't that they were bad people necessarily, only that they didn't belong here. We had a couple of very high-level people, very high-level performers, producing huge financial returns, but they refused to work as a team worker. They were like, "Leave me alone, I'll do my work, stop bothering me." Well, we fired them. And people within the organization were shocked. They were like, "Wait a minute, I thought you said that performance was what counted." I told them that that was only one dimension of what it means to be successful at IBM.

People began to understand that the measuring system was broader than just making money.

Q: Tell a little bit about the customer and how important that is for business today?

A: I don't know how you can be an effective CEO if you don't spend a large amount of time with your customer. You can do that in a number of ways, but the most important way is face-to-face, and not just face-to-face with the customer who lives down the street and who you play golf with every weekend. It has to be a continual reaching out to the customer you've not reached before.

Secondly, I think it's very important to have sophisticated systems that allow you to know what the customer thinks about you and your company. One of the interesting things that happened to me when I got to IBM was that here was IBM going down the tubes, losing market share, losing lots of money, so I said, "Get me the customer satisfaction surveys right away, I want to find out what is going on." So I get these surveys and they come back that IBM was perfect, just wonderful. That can't be. So I was running around, and finally, after four months I said, "Wait a minute, tell me how you do these surveys."

• •

ON THE COFFEE TABLE

The Economist

• •

Well, we go out to our sales force and ask them to tell us the names of some of the customers that they'd like to have surveyed. So the sales people would pick the customer. Then I discovered that they would say to the customer, "You don't have to fill this out, I'll fill this out for you."

We basically abandoned that system. Now we have a system that measures 30,000 customers in a blind survey across eight countries four times a year. Another eight or 10 are semi-annual. It's extremely valuable to get the feedback. It became a starting point for everything we do in the company.

Everything starts with the customer. Number one, the market is the driving force behind everything we do. It's not what *we* like. It's not what *we* did last year. The market is the driving force behind everything we do. There must be contact with the customer, but it must be followed up with a highly sophisticated customer-driven support system that involves a lot of people throughout the organization. Listen. Execute. And execution is a day-to-day activity, and for the most part, top management is not involved.

Q: Any secrets on how you grow a large company, particularly in a challenging market?

A: You've got to have people who think, "Golly, we've got 80 percent of the market, let's go get the other 20 percent." Growth is a mindset. How do I create opportunities? How do I expand the boundaries of what we're going after? That's when a $100 billion market becomes a $300 billion market because you've thought about it differently. There are lots of ways to expand the definition of a market. And then, you've got to make sure that the resources are being allocated to develop the new market.

A lot of people think that business follows the Darwinian theory of the survival of the fittest. In large companies, the Darwinian rule is survival of the fattest. The big divisions generate the products, they generate all the cash, they generate all the revenue. They keep all the money. We always had about six major corporate growth initiatives at IBM and we funded them at corporate. We knew if we had the operating companies fund them, the first month that they got in trouble with their budgets, they were going to get killed.

We funded billion-dollar projects, and we allowed hundreds of millions in losses to accumulate while we were building these new businesses. It's hard to incubate new businesses in an existing company. You have to think about how to make sure it gets the right resources, not just money, but talent and support. Too many times, in my opinion, when companies can't find growth in their base business, they find growth through acquisition. An acquisition strategy works only if it's an implementation arm of some strategy that you really believe in.

Q: What's your advice for that young student who's entering an engineering program at a major university this

fall? Someone like yourself, perhaps, but a few decades younger?

A: A few decades younger? You're very polite. I'm delighted and love to see more young Americans go into engineering and science. It is scary to me that the numbers are declining. And there are a lot of efforts underway to get more people into science.

My advice to somebody going into that field is the same advice I'd give to any young person going into a university: see this as an incredibly important time in your life to build skills. But at the baccalaureate level, I would urge them to reach out as broadly as they can. Learn a foreign language. Learn to appreciate great books. Learn to understand the civic challenges we face in our democracy. I really believe that breadth is important for an undergraduate. I understand that some people can't afford another year or two to go on and get a technical degree but as much as you can, pick up the technical degree. But pick up a broad background as well.

11

❊Success Needs Vision

Dean Butler, *Founder, LensCrafters*

Sometimes business innovation is as much about serendipity as it is about opportunity; as much about risk as commitment. A good example is Dean Butler, who co-founded LensCrafters and pioneered the concept of "Eyeglasses in an Hour." Three decades ago he had a friend who had inherited a chain of eyeglass offices, and the friend needed some advice.

Within a few years, Butler would leave his job at the Procter & Gamble Co. to open an eyeglass company. But first, he had to buck the eyeglass industry titans that fought him in the courts over whether he could manufacture glasses. He eventually won and finally created a revolutionary company with outlets in shopping centers and strip malls. The concept went global and Butler became an international mogul of lenses through LensCrafters, and later, Vision Express.

Question: Tell me about the innovation involved with LensCrafters. How did it all happen?

Answer: I was just a P&G brand manager, like about 10,000 others who have gone through P&G. I had a friend back in 1973 who was a P&G field sales manager, and he inherited his wife's family business, five little optical stores. Back in those days, if you had a good job at Procter & Gamble, you didn't leave because you would be banished for life. His wife's family wanted him to quit his job and run this little family business down in Baton Rouge. He was loath to do it, but he was pressured. I was talking to him about two years later, and he said he knew he shouldn't have done it because they went and changed all the laws.

• •

CDs in the Changer

Endless Summer by The Beach Boys

Greatest Hits by Queen

California Project by Papa Doo Run Run (Brian Wilson)

Sergeant Pepper by The Beatles

• •

In 1976 to 1977, two major things happened. Professional associations could no longer prohibit members from advertising. The second big thing was that anybody who wrote an optical prescription had to give you a copy of it, and then you could go where you wanted to get your glasses. Up until those days, there were very few places where you could advertise eyeglasses. Texas was the only place that had real commercial optical retail development. A Texas company was going to build a store in Baton Rouge, move into my friend's territory, and he panicked.

He didn't know anything about advertising, but I knew a little bit about it. I wrote some commercials for him, acted in them, and produced them because it was the cheapest way to do it. We start advertising on TV and took his monthly sales from $38,000 to $164,000 in six months and did it in the face of competition. We were surprised. We were trying to protect the business, not quadruple it. What I got out of it was free eyeglasses. That was it.

• •

BOOKS ON THE NIGHTSTAND

The World of the Country House in
Seventeenth Century England **by J. T. Cliffe**

The Silk Road, Art and History **by Jonathan Tucker**

The Rainhill Trials: The Greatest Contest of Industrial Britain
and the Birth of Commercial Rail **by Christopher McGowan**

• •

One day he sold the business, but before he left, I asked, "How do you make lenses?" The guy showed me, and I was flabbergasted at how simple it was. It is really straight-forward, a machine-tool process. And what struck me was that the vast majority of eyeglasses are made in 11 or 12 minutes. So I wondered, "Why do you have to wait two weeks?" And then I said, "Somebody ought to put new machines in a store."

We ran some numbers and figured you had to make 21 pair of glasses in a day to break even and since the average optician sold four pairs a day, we realized it was not feasible, that you couldn't do it. So, I forgot about it.

My friend sells his business and two years later he calls me on the phone and wants to meet me in Newark, N.J. I'm like, "I'd love to see you, but Newark?" He said some guy there was doing what I said he should have done. He had put the machines in a store and he had a phenomenal business. We spent a couple hours looking around until they kicked us out. That's when I said they were missing the boat. He was providing glasses in 48 hours. Someone needed to do a while-you-wait service.

Q: Talk about the "while-you-wait" concept.

A: I remember saying that if you can make glasses in a half hour or less, why wait for 48 hours? It was two trips for the customer, a hassle. In those days, optical shops were nine-to-five, closed on Wednesday and open half-a-day on Saturday. I remembered from my P&G stats that 54 percent of American women worked outside the home, and most men. So how do you go see these guys? People thought, too, that this was a saturated category because 50 percent of all the optical products sold in the world were sold in the United States. Well, I didn't think so.

So my friend had no interest of getting back in the industry, but two weeks later he calls me and has an architect on the phone. He wants to build a while-you-wait store and wants me to do the marketing. As for the name, I looked in the telephone book in Cincinnati and back then there was a waterbed store called Mattress Masters. We came up with EyeMasters and it's a big chain today. We opened and, literally, immediately, we were doing 40 jobs a day—not 21.

Q: Double break-even . . .

A: That's right, a ton of money because the raw materials that go into a pair of eyeglasses is less than 20 percent of what is charged. Lenses that are $69 can cost just 50 cents. Contact lenses are even worse. Frequent replacement lenses cost about $13 a six-pack wholesale. Doctors charge $39. And it costs the manufacturer about five cents each—one of the great consumer rip-offs! So the store was doing phenomenally well. And not even in a shopping mall, in a strip center.

CARS IN UK COLLECTION

1938 Maserati 8CTF; 1931 Miller FWD; 1934 MGK3; 1948 Talbot GP; 1912 Mercer Raceabout: 1953 Allard JR; 1953 Studebaker Carerra PanAmericana; 1963 Ford Flathead Dragster, 1963 Scirocco BRM F1; 1968 Camaro Z28 Trans Am Racer; 1935 Diamond T Pickup; 1955 Cadillac Sedan; 1935 MG NA RAC Rally; 1934 ERA R1A; 1951 Indy Roadster *"Jim Robbins Special"*

So after a few months of watching this, I thought, "Gee, I should open one of those." So I quit my job at Procter & Gamble in September 1982 and, by February of 1983, we opened the first LensCrafters in a Kentucky mall. We were afraid to go into a mall, actually, because the rents were so high. The other one was in a strip center. Both stores did great. We started expanding radially: Columbus, Louisville. Phil Barach **[former U.S. Shoe president Philip G. Barach]** heard about us and kept coming to see me, claiming I had a "black box."

• •

FAVORITE CONDIMENT

Thai Chili Sauce
• •

U.S. Shoe was expanding like crazy back in those days. It was hard to do anything wrong. They wanted to buy our business, so finally, I took a five-year deal to run it and got a percentage of the profits. The business was way bigger than they ever imagined. They would never have given me the deal if they knew how big the business was going to be.

Q: It seems to me that P&G prepares people very well for the painstaking step-by-step process of developing and marketing new products. That doesn't lead one to think that this is a very innovative and nimble company, yet they've done some very innovative and nimble product development over the years.

A: Procter & Gamble comes up with product innovation after product innovation after product innovation. A lot are failures, but the world never knows about them. Pampers fell flat on its face the first time they introduced it. They withdrew it from the market. The only way you find out if something is going to work is to go out and test it.

Procter has the guts to do that. There's very little market research you can do that will tell you anything about whether a new product or approach will succeed. You can research consumer experience. You can find out what consumers think about a product they've used, but it is difficult to accurately find out what consumers think about a product they've never used. You are researching something that doesn't exist.

Q: What's the solution for companies that want to be nimble, organizations that want to be innovative?

A: You have to develop a product that consumers never ask for, but when they experience it, they think it's fantastic. It's true of so many P&G products. Find the latent desire. How do you sell a product where there is no inherent interest? That's what I learned to do at Procter & Gamble. Who is interested in laundry detergents? Not particularly anybody. The Brits have a great term; they call it a grudge purchase. You have to buy it. You have to buy glasses, laundry detergent. The vast majority of people who use eyeglasses, use them because they have to use them. They have no particular interest in them at all. They didn't buy them because they are fashionable, or fun to wear. How many people buy toilet tissue because they love to buy toilet tissue? Well, Procter & Gamble has sold a lot of White Cloud and Charmin toilet tissue over the years because they figured out how to sell a product in which there is no inherent interest.

12

✺Discovery

Tom Kelley, *IDEO*

Idea man Tom Kelley is the general manager of product development firm IDEO, the nation's largest industrial-design firm, an outfit that created Apple's first mouse, the sleek Palm V handheld computer, Nike's wraparound sunglasses and Crest's stand-up toothpaste tube. For Kelley, the genesis of most new products and ideas will always be linked to the process of shopping, where a "discovery" is made by the consumer as to their needs or desires. Consumer discovery, which can lead to consumer action, should always be the goal of any astute retailer or product manufacturer.

Question: These are almost always lousy questions but could you name a couple of components of a creative

approach either to a process of shopping or a product?

Answer: I have the experience of the "outside world" —that is, consulting to companies that are doing things the regular way—contrasted with the experience of Ideo, while working on very successful projects. What distinguishes Ideo from the programs that live inside of big corporations is the idea of getting away from your desk.

• •

CDs in the Changer

Grammy nominees 2001 & 2002 by **Various Artists**

Lover's Rock by **Sade**

Drops of Jupiter by **Train**

Paint the Sky with Stars by **Enya**

• •

In spite of some enlightened approaches, there is still this idea around that people who are hunkered down at their desks are doing something—you can't see exactly what they are doing, but they look diligent—which will win you points with some managers. But really, the opposite is true. Knowledge, learning, or insight comes to a company when people get away from a desk and get out in the real world to watch real-life people in their real settings. The trick is to observe where these people stumble, where they have trouble with the status quo. That's where the big opportunities lie.

Consumers won't tell you. They won't raise their hands and say, "You know what I really need is a thing on my front door that lets me know who's there before they knock." Consumers aren't thinking up things for you to make for them. But if you watch someone going in or out of their front door or you watch them brushing their teeth, you'll see stuff. And when you see the stuff, you will think, "Oh, there's some kind of problem." Nobody is talking about it. Nobody is raising their hand. We would say, "Do some field work. Get away from your desk."

Q: As I understand it, the 3M Co. makes a gesture in that direction: the fifteen percent initiative. Researchers must

spend fifteen percent of their time away from their desk.

A: That's right, and they've been very successful, though I've heard recently that they've been cutting into that program. But the 3M approach is slightly different than ours. When they get away from their desks, they're really going from their desk into a research lab and working with chemicals and processes. It's an extension of the desk. Our getting away from the desk is watching customers—or non-customers, as the case may be—and seeing where they have trouble.

Q: Any other examples?

A: I can go on. It's my favorite topic. Here's another one. The battery in my watch wears out so I go into the watch repair shop and wait in line to get the battery replaced. There are several people in front of me in line. I was not hoping for a line in the repair shop but there it was. And guess what? No one in front of me in line had a watch repair. Everybody in line was having their watch battery replaced. It suddenly occurred to me, name another consumer electronic product where you have to go to a specialist and wait in line to get the battery replaced!

If I'm Timex or Nike or Fossil or whoever makes watches and I see a line in the watch repair shop, I'm thinking...

Q: Opportunity...

A: A major opportunity. And the reason the watch repair shop does that is to sell you something else. But if I'm Nike or Timex, I don't want opportunities for watch repair shops; I want an opportunity for my watch, my brand.

- -

BOOKS ON THE NIGHTSTAND

Good to Great: Why Some Companies Make the Leap ...And Others Don't by James C. Collins

Hare Brain Tortoise Mind by Guy Claxon

Weird Ideas that Work by Robert I. Sutton

Cryptonomicon by Neal Stephenson

- -

Q: So intuitive solutions are sometimes not very intuitive at all? Observe the problem and the solution becomes obvious?

A: I would say that compared to finding the problem, finding a solution becomes obvious. And finding the problem is not that hard if you're willing to get out there on the street and watch people. We have specialists who do this—people with PhD's in cognitive psychology and cultural anthropology, and they are 100 times better than I am at it. But we mere mortals can do this too. If you get out and look, you will find something. The risk to describing this is that it sounds kind of obvious.

• •

ON THE COFFEE TABLE

Fast Company, Business Week, InStyle, Time, National Geographic

• •

There is a woman at Harvard Business School, Dorothy Leonard, who says, "Yes, this does sound a bit obvious but very few companies are doing it." I have to say that when I first encountered this, I was a little skeptical. It sounded like a fun and easy job. I didn't get it at first. I would say [that] I'm now 180 degrees different. I would say it is the biggest source of innovation at our firm. This is where you get the spark that tells you what to do next.

Q: I guess it's not unusual for consumer product specialists to furtively watch how shoppers shop but many companies have not embraced the process. How do you get folks at the bottom of the totem pole to embrace the approach? A mandate? Isn't this something that requires individual initiative, that is, you have to want to do it?

A: Here's what I would say. Mandates from the top are not as effective. For those at the top of the organization, I would say this—don't give a mandate, give an invitation. Let people know that it's okay to do this. You cannot force creativity; much of management is getting out of the way and giving people permission, literal or figurative, to do something that's a little bit weird, a little bit off the norm. There are very few companies in America that get this. It's an incredibly powerful tool. It gives vision and it gives power.

At our firm, we do videography and photography. You come back and talk to a client and say, "Gee, you know, people don't know which product to buy." They say, "Forget it. Everybody knows."

And then you throw down 24 digital photographs of people getting lost, or going up to a product and then walking away, or opening a cap and smelling it and scrunching up their face—whatever it is that you've observed. And that data gives you permission to take a point of view.

13

✳Motivate Generations

Claire Raines, *Claire Raines Associates*

Claire Raines sees generational motivation as a critical challenge for firms looking to thrive in the next decade. Choosing the right person for the right job becomes even more critical when dealing with members of the X-Generation. That demographic has no qualms about quietly moving on to another company if their needs are not being met at the company where they are currently employed.

Her client roster includes Microsoft, Toyota, American Express and Sprint.

Question: Do generations get along at work?
Answer: Oh, that's sort of like asking whether people get

along. Yeah, sometimes, but I think there's an awful lot of judging going on—where people don't agree with other people's work ethic or their approach to work and sometimes don't realize it's generational. Sometimes, I think, there's actually quite a bit of generational conflict.

• •

CDs in the Changer

Back on Top by Van Morrison

Keb' Mo' by Keb' Mo'

Brand New Day by Sting

Best of Friends by John Lee Hooker

• •

Q: Is it an older generation judging the younger generation?

A: Partly. Certainly we've had lots of judgment going on by the Baby Boomers [Americans born from 1946 to 1964] of the Generation X-ers [1965 to 1977] for the last 10 or 12 years. But now that the Generation X-ers are established in the work force —they're now 40 percent of the work force and the Boomers are 45 percent—they're getting to be almost as big a group, and they are moving into positions of more control and power. They are also getting more experience and are beginning to say, "Just a minute, this isn't fair. There are all sorts of things about you guys that aren't so wonderful, either." Like Generation X-ers would tell you, Boomers tend to be really political and have learned how to say all the right things like, "We really care what employees think," that kind of stuff.

Q: So boomers have artifice down pat?

A: Right. Generation X-ers think Boomers are artificial, and they think Boomers have been badly indulged, that they've been in the spotlight. Another big complaint that Generation X-ers have is that Boomers are just driven by work, that they've made it the meaning of life, almost like a religion. Generation X-ers think that's pretty unhealthy.

I've been working with this stuff for 15 years. I've written four books about the generations in the workplace based on focus groups, interviews, surveys and lots of other people's work, too. I hope that people will realize that growing up in a different era tends to make people see the world differently, and that that's not a bad thing. I would like executives and corporate leaders to realize that people are not going to grow up and be just like them, that people will get more tolerant of differences and begin to value differences. I would hope people will improve their communications and management styles and keep generational differences in mind.

Q: When it comes to retention, it seems like Generation X-ers are a freelance generation—24 months at a place and they're out of there. That would be heresy to some earlier generations.

A: Absolutely. That is a huge generational difference. Generation X-ers were shaped by the 1970s. They saw an oil shortage and Nixon go down in disgrace. They watched their parents get out-placed and laid off. They grew up in an uncertain economy. They tend to think of themselves first—of course there are all sorts of people who don't fit this profile— but one typical characteristic of Generation X-ers is that they think of themselves as free agents. They think of themselves as marketable commodities.

· ·
BOOKS ON THE NIGHTSTAND

On Writing by Stephen King

Bird by Bird by Anne Lamott

Reading Lolita in Tehran by Azar Nafisi
· ·

Meredith Bagby, the CNNfn reporter, sometimes quotes a survey that says there are more Generation X-ers who believe in UFOs than [those] who believe that Social Security will be there for them. They feel like their only ticket to security is themselves and their resumés.

Q: For employers to retain Generation X-ers—is it a simple question of more dollar signs?

A: Dollar signs work for all the generations, really. For Generation X-ers, money is important, but they also say they want to get that resumé strong, not necessarily because they want to take the resumé somewhere else, but because they want to be developed.

· ·

ON THE COFFEE TABLE

Vanity Fair, People, Creative Nonfiction

· ·

14

☀Public Speaking

Jessica Selasky, *President, Confidence Builders International*

Jessica Selasky and her mother, Dorothy Lynn, owners of Confidence Builders, have traveled the United States to lecture on public speaking and share with companies and executives what is critical for a great speech, short pitch or lengthy presentation. Their company was created when Lynn broke away in 1983 from the American Management Association, where she worked in the President's Association, a division dedicated to teaching the principles of management. She worked closely with CEOs in the program and was steeped in the philosophy of guest speakers that included management gurus like Peter Drucker, Warren Bennis and Herb Cohen.

Selasky started the credit division for Federated

Department Stores Inc., but found that growing the telemarketing department from 13 employees to 200 was unfulfilling. She joined her mother's firm in 1994, which was renamed Confidence Builders International, and the mother-daughter team now offers public presentation coaching and team-tuning to entrepreneurs and large organizations.

CDs in the Changer

It Has to be You by Rod Stewart

Feels Like Home by Norah Jones

Question: Public speaking, even if it's a presentation among colleagues in a conference room at work, is a horrible prospect for most people. Why?

Answer: People are just afraid that they're going to look stupid. There was an article in the *New York Times* that was recently published that found 40 percent of Americans are terrified of public speaking, and that's a real career stopper. People who don't communicate don't get ahead and don't get promoted. People are terrified because they are afraid that somebody in the audience is going to know that the speaker doesn't know anything. In reality, the person who is going to make a speech usually knows more about the topic than they need to know.

Q: Often, when people speak at a convention or seminar, the folks they're talking to are going to be working their way through dessert or salad. They're going to be eating. What can be done to rise above the clinking of the silverware?

A: When you are doing a dinner, lunch or breakfast meal like that, you have to acknowledge that food is being served. You can't pretend that it's not happening. You have to let people eat. But make your presentation a little more light-hearted. Use a little more humor, more stories. Acknowledge that people are eating but do not be afraid of it. A lot of people are intimidated and stutter or stop talking when they hear all that clinking going on.

What we really preach is to be natural and let your gestures come naturally, that you shouldn't pre-plan gestures. Our teaching goes against the grain. A lot of people who teach public speaking think you should memorize your presentation, write the speech down word for word, write down your gestures, where you're going to make them. We say don't do any of that.

Q: Why do you break from that tradition?

A: We believe you don't want to write the speech, memorize it and tell jokes. We're not joke tellers. What you should do is be natural, be prepared and be enthusiastic. If you say big, your hands go to big. You don't have to pre-think that. We really believe in extemporaneous speaking. Be natural. Be prepared. Be enthusiastic. Those are the three points we talk about. That's how you overcome that nervousness, too. Those are the three keys: be natural, prepared, enthusiastic.

Q: I know one of your tips is that if you see attention flagging, announce, "Let me tell you a story," and you'll get the audience's complete attention because everybody likes a story. Any other tips?

A: Yes. Just pause or be silent for a moment. That makes people uncomfortable and will bring their attention back up to you. Also, use humor. Really fantastic speakers are the ones who use humor. Our motto is laughter precedes learning.

• •

BOOKS ON THE NIGHTSTAND

The Lords of Discipline by Patrick Conroy

Death By Meeting by Patrick Lencioni

• •

Q: But isn't humor a risk—that it's not going to be funny? What if it lands flat and nobody gets it?

A: Yes, it is, and you have to be careful with it. It should be something having to do with the moment. Remember that audiences want you to succeed. Every audience wants you to succeed. And they give you a certain amount of time at the beginning of the speech to let you succeed. If you're still acting nervous after 30 seconds, maybe two minutes, that's when they'll turn on you.

• •
BOOKMARKS

www.humorproject.com
• •

Q: Note cards? Yes or no.

A: Yes, we believe in extemporaneous speaking. You know what you're going to say, so we suggest picking out key ideas that you want to get across. Write single words or short phrases on note cards, for instance, the word "planning." Well, you know what you're going to say about planning so you don't have to write down everything you're going to say. Put maybe 10 key points on your card and that's all you're going to need.

At some point in your life, you have had to make a speech and felt very uncomfortable or your friends made fun of you or your teacher said you should have done this or done that—and all of a sudden, the fear is there. It's hard to overcome. Visualization is great. Visualize yourself enjoying the moment. We don't want to teach people how to speak in public. We want to teach people how to speak in public and how to enjoy it and be present in the moment. That's our goal.

15

✳Create Your Boss

Peter Block, *Author, "Flawless Consulting"*

Peter Block, a partner in Designed Learning, in Mystic, Conn., revolutionized the world of consulting with his book *Flawless Consulting,* which has sold more than 700,000 copies since its release in 1979. It informs companies and executive coaches how to deal effectively with clients, peers and the workforce, and offers strategies on how to bring about change at multiple levels in an organization.

Block has been on the edge of the management curve in the workplace for decades with his premise that individual and collective action can lead to wholesale changes in the workplace, but only if groups are treated as collections of individuals and only if individuals are offered authentic options. As author and consultant, Block focuses on restoration of community and development of organizations. He has written six books, and his *The Answer to How Is Yes: Acting on What Matters* (Berrett-Koehler) won the 2002 Independent Book Publisher Award for Business Breakthrough Book of the Year.

Question: As I understand it, you now suggest that while there is plenty of so-called "teaching" going on at work, there is precious little learning. Are people still too dependent upon letting others define what they need to learn?

Answer: Totally. It's the nature of work. People are treating their bosses as if they are more important than other workers, rather than what they are—just bosses. Most people are afraid.

• •

CDs in the Changer

With a Little Help from my Friends by **Joe Cocker**

Time Out of Mind by **Bob Dylan**

Classics, Vol.13 by **Nils Lofgren**

From Bessie to Brazil by **Susannah McCorkle**

Room to Breath by **Delbert McClinton**

• •

Q: Why is it so difficult to get people to understand that change can be good for them, good for their organization, even good for society?

A: Change is painful. And it usually comes at a time of crisis. Change is usually brought about by coercion—soft-core coercion. It's called *mandate* or people are busy *installing change.* Plus everybody wants to change somebody else. The only people who talk about change being difficult are the ones being forced to change. Nobody complains about the changes they are choosing for themselves. So most change at institutions is of a coercive or colonial nature. We all think if somebody else changed, we would be all right. We would be better. This is the myth of institutional life: *Those people are the problem.*

Q: Isn't fear of imminent punishment a powerful force? Isn't coercion effective?

A: I don't think so. It creates enormous resistance. They've done studies as to which is more motivating—telling people what is possible and rewarding them, or punishing them. What punishment does is tell you what not to do. It's not really learning. It's more like paralysis. Most institutions that embrace a reward/punishment system are under the illusion that it motivates people. Most people don't need to be motivated. It's a lot of mythology.

Q: So people are hard-wired to do the right thing?

A: Well, they are hard-wired in both directions. They are hard-wired to find out what's possible, to do the right thing, to be useful. But they are also hard-wired to surrender their freedom. It's a complicated wiring system. You have a choice as to what you want to see when you look out there. Do you want to see that people long to do something meaningful or do you want to see that people are willing to surrender their freedom and avoid responsibility? Both are true. Why not speak to the part that wants to create meaning? Especially once people grow up a little bit.

Q: I surmise you are not a big fan of performance reviews, formal appraisals, and the like. Could you sum up why?

A: I just think they are punitive and demeaning. They just reinforce the fact that somebody has sovereignty. I don't think they facilitate learning. Most people are so anxious in a performance review, they don't know what they are saying and don't know what they are hearing. They avoid them. Managers hate giving them, and subordinates hate receiving them. The A-students never mind getting graded, but everybody else, you almost have to threaten people to hold them. Most personnel departments say if you don't turn in your performance appraisals, none of your people are getting any increases. Why do we have to go to those extremes?

I think the appraisal itself is part of the problem. People don't perform well because they are cautious, wary. They are afraid, if not of their boss, then of their boss' boss. It's no excuse, though. The other side of the story is that people are responsible for how they are inside the institution. Subordinates create the bosses that they have.

Q: Subordinates create the bosses they have?

A: You decide how autocratic or understanding your boss is by how you relate to them and the expectations you have. When people complain to me about how their boss doesn't listen, doesn't support or doesn't develop them, I always say, well, why are you creating a boss like that? And why would you want those things from a boss?

There are lots of places to get support. There are lots of places to learn. Why do we put all this energy into a boss? Inside an institution, if you want to be appraised, ask your peers how you are doing. They are usually harder to fool. Bosses are easier to fool. You manipulate your boss by saying, "Thank you, that was helpful" or "I'm working on it."

· ·

BOOKS ON THE NIGHTSTAND

I Bought Andy Warhol by **Richard Polsky**

The Careless Society by **John McKnight**

No Word from Winifred by **Amanda Cross**

The Future of Freedom by **Fareed Zakaria**

The Process of Creating Life by **Christopher Alexander**

· ·

If negative feedback helped, why are we still getting the same feedback today as we got from people 10 years ago? Most of the time when you say something negative, people say, "Oh yeah, my partner told me that, my boss told me that, I've been hearing that for years." Well, that tells me that maybe that conversation isn't a useful conversation. Part of the challenge is to create conversations. If you're interested in change or development, here is a great question: What's the conversation that we haven't had?

Q: Why has *Flawless Consulting* touched such a chord among American business owners and others?

A: I don't know. I think it's some kind of an unusual mixture of spirit and practicality. I wrote it to seduce engineers and IT people into caring about relationships. It's written with boxes, lines, steps, lists and guides. That's the allure—it's very concrete and very specific. It's specific about being authentic, and it's specific about elusive ideas.

Somehow that book brought the centrality of relationships into the consulting business. That's where people get into trouble. Most people giving advice aren't wrong. They just ignore the relationship or take it lightly. Same with managers, most of the advice or direction that managers give is not wrong, it's just that they have no connection or relationship with the people they are directing, so that advice is not heard. When I wrote it, I was embarrassed by it. I only wrote it because I had a contract.

Q: Get out of here ...

A: I'm serious. When I wrote it, I was 40 years old. I gave a talk. I never wanted to write it. A guy came up to me and said, "You want to write a book about this?"

I said, "I've never written a book."

He says, "Well, I'll give you some money if you write a book." So I signed the contract because he gave me a guarantee and when I finished the book, I thought, "Oh God, I hope none of my colleagues read it." I don't get it. I don't sell them. I don't promote the books at my speeches. It sells more now than it did 20 years ago. Figure that out.

16

❀Gender Violence

Paul Charron, *Liz Claiborne*

Paul Charron, chairman and chief executive of Liz Claiborne Inc., a New York City-based Fortune 500 company, is a pioneer in raising awareness about the problem of domestic violence and its impact on the workplace. Charron's challenge is to convince other executives that domestic violence impacts productivity and morale and, finally, profits—no matter the size of the company, its location or product.

Question: Domestic violence is something that happens in the home, not in the workplace. Why should companies do something?
Answer: Domestic violence or relationship violence

is really a business issue. It leads to absenteeism. It leads to higher health costs. It adversely affects productivity. As far as I'm concerned, those are business issues, and I've got to get to the root cause.

• •

CDs in the Changer

The Soundtrack from Mama Mia: The Musical Based on the Songs of ABBA

The Doo Wop Box: Vintage Rock and Roll by Various Artists
No Fences by Garth Brooks

• •

I believe very strongly in and would like to take credit for initiating my company's role in domestic violence, though, in truth, it was my predecessor, Jerry Chazen, who started our involvement in this program in 1991. When I came in here in 1994, I took an ax to a lot of things in the cost area. I got rid of a number of people because we were definitely in a turn-around mode. I was going to get rid of this program, but had the good sense to listen to a lot of persuasive people, who told me that they thought I was making a big mistake. The good news is that I deferred to their judgment and, subsequently, came over to their side. That's one of the reasons why we've stayed front and center on this issue.

Q: If there are 70 million people between the ages of 3 and 17 in the United States, and if there is abuse, both verbal and physical abuse, going on in many of the homes where those children live, a cycle is created that is probably a real challenge to break.

A: You are totally right. We've been very involved in speaking to girls about the possibility of relationship violence and that [they] don't have to put up with this. Violence is a learned behavior. Kids learn it from their parents and pass it on to their children.

There are so many children being born to 19- and 20-year-olds who think this is the way to act. Look at that video where the woman is just throttling this kid—beating the crap out of this 4-year-old kid in the car—and she's very repentant now. But if the camera hadn't caught this lady, she would have done it again. Hopefully, others see this.

The lady said she was just stressed out. Well, if she has a job, do you think she is manifesting that stress in the workplace?

Relationship violence raises this question: Is there anything that could be done or should be done in the environment where people work to determine that violent behavior is about to be triggered? Are there warning signs that somebody could and should pick up on?

. . . .
BOOKS ON THE NIGHTSTAND

Flyboys by James Bradley

The Kills by Linda Fairstein

What the CEO Wants You to Know by Ram Charan
. . . .

What a company like Liz Claiborne is trying to do—we're not psychologists, we're not professional counselors—is to acknowledge what reality is and to try to make the world a better place. We must educate people and make the world a better place by using our creativity, our funding and our bully pulpit.

Q: What can you do from your bully pulpit?

A: This is a big deal for us. This is a discussion that should occur in every community and should get people to acknowledge that this is a societal problem and a business problem. If it's a business problem, then CEOs and companies ought to do something about it. If the CEO says it's going to happen, that this is where a company will focus a portion of their efforts, then by God—it's going to happen. Because, frankly, anything the CEO wants generally takes place.

Q: Tell me about your time with branding, at P&G.

A: P&G gave me a strategic context within which to

evaluate every business issue. It's the foundation, the structure, the framework that I take to the bank every day.

Q: Are you still able to write a one-page memo? Do you need to write one-page memos?

A: Hah, when I was there we wrote plenty of one-page memos, and I communicate in writing very succinctly and send a lot of thought-pieces to my associates. They rarely exceed one page. I find that the written word is more easily understood. The written memorandum of direction or sharing insight is something that I can refer to in subsequent days and weeks as a reminder of what I said, what I was thinking and it enables me to supervise a broad span of control.

ON THE COFFEE TABLE

Forbes, Fortune and *InStyle*

I think the second thing P&G gave me was a reflexive competency in marketing. I always wanted to be a general manager; general managers have a distinctive competency in key areas—marketing, finance, administration or whatever—and are really good in one or two areas. They have no fatal flaws, no areas that they're awful in.

Procter gave me a reflexive competency in marketing that I also take to the bank every day. I know intuitively and by training what to do in marketing. At least I feel I do. That's half the battle. Those two important learnings influenced the executive I've become. I would also say that I was fortunate to have many high-quality mentors at P&G.

People at P&G are intelligent but what makes P&G great is the universality of the system: the checklist, the consistency of the approach and the discipline.

17

❀Innovate

Michael L. Tushman, Ph.D, *Harvard Business School, MIT, Cornell University*

When people at a company embrace innovation or change, that company is more likely to find long-term success, says Michael L. Tushman, Ph.D., an expert on innovation.

A professor of Business Administration at the Graduate School of Business at Harvard University, Tushman has worked for more than a decade on analyzing why short-term success can turn into long-term failure. He holds degrees from Northeastern University (B.S.E.E.), Cornell University (M.S.), and the Sloan School of Management at M.I.T. (Ph.D.) His client list includes Bristol-Meyers Squibb, GE, Hewlett-Packard and Merck.

Question: Corporate innovation is sometimes a euphemism for cannibalization, companies eating their young. Some companies and executives must be nervous about innovation, looking at it with a sense of impending danger.

Answer: Companies should look at it as dangerous not to innovate. I look at innovation with colleagues and students through a notion of a stream of innovation. First, there's bigger and better—that is, an incremental change. There are also architectural changes and radical changes. Radical change is something quite discontinuous and substitutional: radial tires substituting for bias-ply tires. Or take the quartz watch. The watch industry went through radical change to a completely different customer set.

We believe that dynamic capabilities at the firm level are anchored and played out in that innovation space. We argue that firms need to think about different types of innovation; some of these lead to substitution, but most do not. Most are complementary. Take the quartz watch example. The Swatch Group now is selling an awful lot of mechanical watches, the old-fashioned, very expensive mechanical watches. They haven't given that up.

Yes, innovation can be cannibalization, like the radial tire, which really did cannibalize the existing bias-ply tire franchise, but most innovations in this innovation stream are not.

Q: The challenge, then, is to enable innovation.

A: The way we describe it is to create organizations that celebrate exploitative behavior. I don't mean exploiting employees, but rather exploiting your existing competencies, as well as celebrating and honoring exploratory behavior. There must be lots of experiments, even though many will fail. Some will be the future of the franchise. That ability to both explore and exploit simultaneously is a fundamental insight into building an ambidextrous structure, what we call an "ambidextrous form."

Q: Let's talk about Vinnie Bagadonuts, V.P. of Operations. He has a widget fastener factory floor with 90 people and sees a distant future where consumers may no longer need widget fasteners. Where does he start?

A: Vinnie Bagadonuts, if he's on the factory floor, depends upon his R&D crowd to come up with a new fastener. He has to have his production factory floor continue to do the existing fastener and then learn this new fastening approach.

There are diagnostic abilities that are important. He must look at the competencies of his 40 people, their raw skills and abilities. He needs to look at the culture on his factory floor and see if it is open to new streams of innovation, open to collaboration with colleagues in marketing and R&D.

Finally, does he manage the processes on his factory floor in a way that will increase the probability that he can exploit existing skills in fastenings and explore new fastening production techniques? We push Vinnie to look at not only his strategy for his factory floor around these innovation streams, but we also push the Vinnies and their teams to think about their own styles as leaders, their own decision-making practices, so they are able to foster this incremental innovation and the more discontinuous innovation.

Q: I have a feeling that the boss's furrowed brow discourages more innovation than anything else.

A: Oh yeah, absolutely. If Vinnie, a couple of years down the road, sees some new fastening thing, and his boss doesn't get it, the first thing Vinnie has to do is manage the boss. Say, "Hey, Furrowed-brow-boss, you're locked in the past and we have got to get going with this." If the bosses are only focused on cost, there will be no innovation.

Q: What business structures tend to foster innovation?

A: You're on to a key point. The Vinnies of the world cannot foster innovation streams. It has to be Vinnie's boss or Vinnie's boss's boss. The senior team of the fastening organization has to do this. They can't rely on Vinnie to do this because Vinnie is outgunned politically. It has to be the senior team.

But the question is structure. Whether it's Vinnie on the factory floor or Vinnie's general manager in this fastener business, there needs to be an ambidextrous structure, a structure that celebrates inconsistency while it builds systems into the organization. There need to be procedures and controls that focus on costs and efficiency, even as structures are created that celebrate chaos, mistakes, wacky kinds of innovations, and the creation of options.

Those forms are inconsistent so it places a lot of pressure on senior teams who must act consistently inconsistent. Companies must create multiple organizational architectures that both honor exploitation and honor exploration simultaneously. Do you see what I'm saying?

Q: Well, you kind of went Zen on me there, I think. When a guy goes Zen on me, I have to ask, can you do all that?

A: Well, poor Vinnie down on the factory floor is in trouble if management has that furrowed brow. The nub of innovation streams and dynamic capabilities is having senior teams that have a cognitively complex model of their industry and are able to think about substitution, as well as incremental change and then build the requisite organization forms. At some point they'll need to manage change but the more provocative stuff is to build teams that can be ambidextrous

18

❋Women and Work

Sheila Wellington, *Catalyst*

Sheila W. Wellington is the former president of Catalyst, ranked by the American Institute of Philanthropy as the highest rated nonprofit in the nation focusing on women's issues. The organization has consistently broken new ground with its studies of gender in the workplace. From her position, Wellington seized the opportunity to evaluate the corporate workplace for women executives. Today, she is clinical professor of management at the NYU/Stern School of Business.

Question: I know that Catalyst has done some great work on minority women executives—what is the level-set on that effort and where do we go from here?

Answer: We did a very, very large study a few years ago of 1,700 respondents. We had 59 focus groups that we convened across the country. As a research-based organization, the first thing we do is get information about what is really going on. Frequently we have anecdotes or impressions, when we lack real information. Our sense was that when we studied women in corporate America or women in law we were unable to get sufficient numbers of women of color so that we could, in a reliable and statistically valid way, learn or teach anything specific about them.

· ·

CDs in the Changer

Verdi: Rigoletto (Complete Opera)
by Maria Callas, Tito Gobbi and Giuseppe di Stefano

Viva Verdi **by Various Artists**

· ·

We decided to do a study just of women of color in corporate management. It was a very tough study—three years to complete and it cost $300,000. The major findings of that study were, essentially, that women of color spoke of a concrete ceiling, a phrase that I had never heard before. It was a very, very commonly used phrase.

They spoke about what for them were the main barriers. The first one was not having an influential mentor or sponsor. The next was lack of informal networking, then the lack of a company role model. These are the top three, but each are about isolation and exclusion. Just think about it. No mentors, no informal networking with influential colleagues, no role models. It's about not having anybody to learn from. They're walking alone.

This, for us, was very powerful. Women frequently cite absence of a mentor, and we've done similar studies across Europe, Canada and the United States for industry after industry, but never have we had all these factors of isolation and exclusion be the main barriers. This survey was done in the United States. About half of those surveyed were African-

American, a quarter were Asian, and a quarter were Hispanic. So we could compare within the groups.

Q: How do women compensate? Human beings tend to compensate when there's a particular challenge. What are the success factors?

A: High-visibility assignments and performing above expectations. We have one quote from a woman who said it isn't very hard to perform above expectations because expectations for women like her are so low anyway.

· ·

BOOKS ON THE NIGHTSTAND

The Peloponnesian War **by Donald Kagan**

Goodnight Moon **by Margaret Wise Brown**

· ·

Communicating well is another success factor. In the latest study three years ago, we went back to a large sample of these very same women and asked them if we could continue to contact them, and 900 said yes. Now, there is some good news in the re-contact study. The first study got a great deal of coverage, lots of media, and lots of corporate response. Essentially, that study pointed out that here is something that can be talked about.

Q: So corporate America reacted and you came back three years later with another study?

A: Yes. There is some good news and it's very interesting. The good news is that promotion rates and rates of salary increases are roughly the same as they are for white women, and there have been a large number of promotions. Networks formed and women of color actively sought mentors. This is really an interesting finding—of the women of color who were promoted, 50 percent had no mentor. We asked the women who were promoted if they had mentors and learned that 50 percent of the women with no mentors were promoted, 60 percent of the women with one mentor were promoted and 71 percent of the women who had more than one mentor were promoted.

The connection between having a mentor, somebody to give you a helping hand, and getting ahead was simply borne out statistically. This is really a significant finding.

What women of color are doing if they want to get ahead is they are looking for a coach, looking for an advocate; they are looking to play the game.

Q: One of the problems with good research is that it always leads to more questions—what are the questions that have emerged at this point?

A: The research questions we ask these days center on what women of color perceive as their issues and success factors. For one thing, women are less optimistic than they were in the original study. That's the bad news. Either they're getting tired or everybody is less optimistic these days than they were three years ago.

And there's a pyramid. You get a promotion. You look up. There are fewer seats up there. The question corporate America has to ask is, "What do we do about it now?"

The women are learning what they have to do. The questions now are, "What works inside companies? What programs and policies can good companies undertake to make progress?" If this debate plays out woman by woman, it's going to be really slow. Still, there are an awful lot of companies out there that want to tap into all the talent, whatever the race, whatever the gender.

Overall, my feeling is I want this work on my tombstone, I feel so proud of it.

19

✺Communicate

Larry Nadler, PhD.

Larry Nadler is a professor of communication at Miami University, Oxford, Ohio, and a world-renowned specialist in interpersonal communications, particularly gender and it's impact on salary negotiations. Nadler offers insight into how male and female managers and workers interact in the workplace.

Question: Are there any triggers or warning signs about gender bias?

Answer: A good tip-off that an employee is focusing on gender—that the employee is conscious that he or she is talking to a male or female rather than a boss—is shown through nonverbal behavior, like facial expressions.

There is something known as micro-momentary expressions. Those are very brief, a fifth-of-a-second in length, facial expressions that show true feelings. Often employees have to suppress those things. They may be upset with the boss, but they can't let it show or it's insubordination. But really brief facial expressions may leak out that show how they really feel. A manager could pick up disdain or brief expressions of disdain.

And it is not just the face. It could be a subordinate using eye contact. People in role relationships usually use more eye contact than the people in higher positions. Usually, a person in the lower position is expected to show more eye contact. A person disdainful of a female manager shows less eye contact. But how do you take action against somebody who shows a little less eye contact?

Then, for somebody who is gender skeptical, there is tone of voice. It's not the words but the tone that could show less patience, less trust and less respect—not what they say, but how they say it.

Q: What if it is justified, that is, the manager is in over their head?

A: Any manager needs to earn respect and trust of their workers, regardless of gender. Is it the case that women managers have to work harder to earn that respect? Yes. Is that fair or right? No, it's reality. It doesn't always happen, but there's enough of a trend—and the Arizona State study is consistent with others in the field. Truth and honesty in life can be difficult, just as truth and honesty in the workplace can sometimes be a challenge.

Q: Should the female manager confront the employee with "You're not respecting me because I'm a woman"?

A: That's a good and difficult question. The reason it's a tough question to answer is simply because a lot of people say women face "double-binds." A double-bind means that either way you choose, you lose. A lot comes back to sex role stereotypes and expectations. If we're trying to explain why an

Arizona State study produced a finding and why more women managers face unique obstacles, it comes down more than any other factor to sex role stereotypes and expectations.

• •

CDs IN THE CHANGER

Two Against Nature by Steely Dan

Benefit by Jethro Tull

Paranoid by Black Sabbath

• •

For women, the double-bind in our culture is that they have been expected to be nurturing, supportive and dependent upon others, that's the female sex role in our culture. The double-bind is whatever choice a woman makes, there is a cost. If a woman chooses to be nurturing, on one hand they will be fairly well-accepted and liked as a person. But many of those sexual expectations work against her as a manager in the workplace because people tend to think of upper level managers as logical and in control, and the expectations of females run counter to that. The other half of the double-bind is that it might help a woman manager to get ahead in the workplace by being more assertive and logical, but the terminology people use to describe assertive women in our culture is…

Q: It's not Dear Old Mom, is it?

A: No, it rhymes with witch. Either way she chooses, she loses.

So to answer the question, should she confront the employee? You have a double-bind. If she chooses not to, if she just lets it go—conflict avoidance. On the one hand, there's no overt problem, but it is a problem that is not resolved, and the employee will continue to behave that way.

The problem with calling attention to it is you don't know what will happen as a result. If the choice is confrontation, you may win the battle and lose the war. By calling attention to it, the downside is you have addressed one small symptom of the problem—but it may make for a deeper problem. It may boomerang. The employee may deny it. And unless the manager can give concrete examples that verify their point, it opens a can of worms. The employee now goes around to fellow workers and says, "Can you believe her? She is so sensitive, and now she's projecting her insecurities onto me." Anytime a manager confronts an employee about something, they better be able to document it.

. . . .

BOOKS ON THE NIGHTSTAND

Eight Simple Rules for Dating my Teenage Daughter
by W. Bruce Cameron

Nighttime is My Time by Mary Higgins Clark

. . . .

Personally, I think that women managers need to lead by example, by actions rather than words. By treating employees with respect, trusting employees and modeling effective behaviors, the manager will come to gain acceptance.

And there's a large body of research that shows women have better communication skills and can capitalize on that. Women are typically better listeners. They are often more empathetic toward others. They are often more tactful and considerate. When managing conflict, they often use more pro-social strategies—rewards rather than threats, positive reinforcement, openness to what the other person thinks.

In a sense, a manager is managing two things—the task and relationships. Women in our culture on the whole have very good relational skills. And in the workplace, it's something women managers can capitalize on or utilize to their benefit.

21

❋Loyalty

Richard Barlow, *Frequency Marketing*

Getting customers is always a challenge, but keeping them is twice as hard. The frequency marketing division of Alliance Data Systems Corp. of Dallas, Texas, designs, implements and manages loyalty-marketing programs that reward customers for buying clients' products and services. The company's Loyalty Solutions Platform software creates loyalty programs in about 60 days. Richard G. Barlow is the division's founder, former chairman and chief executive.

Question: What is a common mistake that companies and executives make when attempting to encourage loyalty among their clients or customers?

Answer: The terrain of customer loyalty is a broad one, beginning with customer service, ranging over to the little piece of ground that we map out, the area of structured programs of recognition and rewards. When we talk about customer loyalty, we talk about programs that systematically recognize and reward customers based upon tracking their purchase behavior. Whether it's best customer, preferred customer or loyal customer, there are a number of mistakes that companies make.

CDs in the Changer

The Very Best of the Drifters by The Drifters

Another Place Another Time by Jerry Lee Lewis

Dream With Dean by Dean Martin

Soul Sauce by Cal Tjader

The Look of Love by Diana Krall

The most common mistake is to assume that either end of the equation—the recognition or the reward end of the equation—are sufficient unto themselves. In other words, a company launches a loyalty program that consists only of rewards—hard benefits—or, more commonly, a company launches a program that consists only of recognition, typically in some form of communication or discount structure. These programs, if overly dependent on one component or the other, don't work very well and the longer they exist, the less effective they are.

Q: What are the risks of poor loyalty programs?
A: People tune them out. The challenge of an effective loyalty program is a compelling value proposition—offer the consumer something that is irresistible. If you offer the customer more of your stuff free or more of your stuff discounted, it's boring.

Q: What industry does it well?
A: Airlines do it well, but they have a unique cost and

technology structure that allows them to give away products at a low cost. If I know a seat is going to be empty, I can give it away, and it only costs a few dollars to put a person in the seat—about $16. That's unique. They have something else that is equally important. They have a product loaded with emotional content—a trip on a plane isn't just a trip on a plane, it's an experience, and the context of an experience is emotion. Frequent-flyer miles are uniquely valuable in the mind of the consumer because he sees them as part of a total experience, and travel is the ultimate experience.

BOOKS ON THE NIGHTSTAND

A Short History of Just About Everything by Bill Bryson

Folly & Glory by Larry McMurtry

Stalin: The Court of the Red Tsar by Simon Sebag Montefiore

The Nonpatriotic President: A Survey of the Clinton Years
by Janet Scott Barlow

Not every company, obviously, can do that. Even hotel companies don't have the same capability because the cost structure is so different. Airlines not only have this magical product, but they can add upgrades to the product. When you get upgraded to first class, there is no denying you're special when sitting in that first-class seat, watching people headed to coach.

You must establish a form of added value, separate from the normal product attributes and price list so it is clearly value-added. If it's properly designed, it is distinct and separate from pricing so it is not discount-dependent. Discounts erode margins, erode price and value, and train the customer never to pay full price. You need to look at the nature of the business and figure out what type of added value would differentiate the business from the competition, without hurting margins or the perceived value of the product.

Q: How can companies juice recognition and reward

programs?

A: It is a combination of art and science. First, you have to ask the customer what he likes about current service, what he doesn't like and what he wishes you would do for him to show he's special. It is a much more sophisticated piece of research, but that is the essence—asking the customer what would delight him.

They don't know, but it's a fundamental step you have to cover. You have to check with customers. You may get insight. You will get direction, but you will not get breakthrough. That's where the art comes in because it's not the customer's job to tell you how to delight him. It's your job, and we have a process for that. It examines the emotional opportunities within your brand and uncovers possibilities for delighting the customer through recognition and reward.

Q: What are standout programs?

A: A business-to-business program for Bell Atlantic is a good one. For the past five years, it has been a very effective loyalty program for small and medium business segments.

· ·

FAVORITE MOVIES

The Godfather (I & II)

The Big Lebowski

Late Last Night

· ·

At Bell Atlantic, hundreds of thousands of business customers are enrolled in BusinessLink. The program was based on billings, and a point structure was developed where a customer could redeem bonus credits for specific products and services. The most important component was the business-building rewards—take a customer to lunch. The theory was that if a business redeemed credits, the business would get lunch for two at any of several hundred restaurants. You could take a customer to lunch and build your business. I am restrained by a non-disclosure statement from giving details, but we found that the program was an enormous success.

You would think a small-business owner would do anything he wanted with lunches for two, that there would be a lot of personal use and, no doubt, there was some of that. But the largest kind of use, research uncovered, was that business owners and managers used the lunches as an employee reward. They hosted an employee at lunch, recognized an anniversary or an employee for achieving a goal or maybe it was just a thank you. We broadened the concept into Take a Customer to Dinner, Take a Customer Out on the Town, Take a Customer to the Theater, to a baseball game or to a football game.

It has been extremely successful and allows a business member to build a relationship that is extremely valuable to his company. The trick of a loyalty program is to segment customers and bring each segment some kind of added value in terms of reward and recognition. It will be meaningful to the business.

20

❀Bank On It

Ron DeLyons, *Creekwood Advisors*

"I have a rare opportunity to do well and do good. When you are a capitalist, it's very rare that you have a chance to do both."

—Ron DeLyons

Creating capital, jobs and wealth in emerging American markets promises to be the focus of minority-led firms for at least the next two decades, according to a joint report from the Milken Institute and Ford Foundation.

Investment banker Ron DeLyons is part of that transformation through Creekwood Advisors, a boutique investment banking/buy-out firm specializing in minority-led transactions.

DeLyons created Creekwood after founding Greystone Investment Management in 1999. Currently, while minorities represent 28 percent of the population, they own only 12 percent of firms. Though the number of ethnic-owned firms grew at twice the rate of all firms during the past decade, researchers have found that those companies still face capital gaps and challenges that limit their ability to expand.

Question: You had about $290 million under management at Greystone—and you walked away? Are you delirious?

Answer: Hah! The short answer is there is an opportunity, a supply-demand mismatch where I—based on who I am— have a competitive advantage. As a businessperson, you look for situations where you have a competitive advantage. But more to the point, I have a rare opportunity to do well and do good. When you are a capitalist, it's very rare that you have a chance to do both.

. . . .
CDs in the Changer

Everything Must Go by Steely Dan

Love Story by Vivian Green

Princess Nubiennes by Les Nubians

Breezin' by George Benson

Letter from Home by Pat Metheny

Paid Tha Cost to Be Da Boss by Snoop Dogg
. . . .

The opportunity to do well is driven by economics, that is, to grow a business. The opportunity to do good is driven by the chance to provide opportunities to those who have historically been denied—to develop an organization that from the top down is more reflective of society as a whole. By focusing on supplier diversity initiatives, a competitive minority-owned firm with the capacity to perform on larger contracts has the potential to do both well and good.

Q: Where is the demand opportunity? Are there demographics at play?

A: It's less demographics than it is a function of large corporations understanding the benefits of supplier diversity and spreading the wealth. As our society becomes more diverse, it makes sense to ensure that there are more "haves" than "have-nots." Companies are realizing that consumers are represented by broader society and that there are advantages to inclusion beyond the notion of guilt or reparations. Creekwood is a boutique investment banking firm that specializes in minority-led transactions. As a buyout firm, our goal is to create larger minority-owned firms that are positioned to compete for large contracts, usually serving Fortune 500 companies and government entities. Ideally, we would like to do transactions with companies that have sales in excess of $25 million. What that does is give us the critical mass to deliver on larger contracts to Fortune 500 companies.

Understand there are thousands of minority-owned firms in the state of Ohio alone. But the vast majority of them don't have annual revenues in excess of $500,000. If you're a Toyota or a Procter & Gamble or any large organization that has an objective to do a billion dollars worth of business annually with minority-owned firms, it doesn't take a genius to figure out it's difficult to accomplish that at $200,000 a shot. It's just not possible. The need to increase infrastructure and the lack of customer diversification would make it impractical for the small-business owner to compete.

Q: Are there baby boomer business owners who are looking at their sixties and saying time for me to shut it down and move to that house in North Carolina?

A: That is one place for opportunities—the lack of any succession plan. People are beating the track down to Florida or North Carolina. They've been successful in their businesses and want to slow down and are looking for an exit strategy.

Also, we think there are huge opportunities at the large corporations that have supplier diversity initiatives but also have relatively small subsidiaries—from their perspective—that are non-core assets, something they've picked up through acquisitions from larger firms or they've developed internally.

Q: What is Creekwood? Who are the principals?
A: At this point, it's me. What we do, currently, is work with a board of advisers and, depending upon the industry and transaction, I have several people who assist me and analyze each transaction.

BOOKS ON THE NIGHTSTAND

Exodus by Leon Uris

An Unfinished Life, John F. Kennedy by Robert Dallek

Power Failure – The Inside Story of the Collapse of Enron by Mimi Swartz

Q: In the best of all possible worlds, where will Creekwood be three years out?
A: I would like to have completed at least three or four transactions with total annual sales of $1 billion. Additionally, my goal is to assemble a team of professionals that are representative of our society going forward and ideally, growing the top line by managing costs, providing more job opportunities, more management opportunities that are more reflective of the community as a whole. In 10 years, I would like to exit, leaving the management teams as owners of firms that can compete with or without the advantages of minority ownership.

My background is in investment banking and finance. And I have very smart friends and surround myself with people who are much smarter than I am. If you look at studies, it shows that team decisions are much more effective than individual decisions. I rely very heavily on a group of very successful, smart people who become guides through this maze.

I have personal assets, obviously. I'm not Bill Gates, but I have assets. Additionally, the deals we are looking at are bankable transactions. These are profitable companies. Ideally, what we will do is put together a transaction that might be slightly more leveraged to allow us to close quickly and then syndicate that out to an investment group we are developing that is primarily made up of minorities.

Q: What sectors?
A: We are very, very bullish on the energy sector. Everybody needs energy. Everybody needs power. There are larger contracts for energy, and most of the Fortune 500 companies have large energy needs. My goal is to find an entry point in the energy industry on some level, whether it's renewables, natural gas, marketing, supplying, energy efficiency—there are a lot of areas in the energy space where we can be competitive if we can acquire the right company.

· ·
THINGS I WISH I KNEW AT THE START

Numbers don't lie, people do.

Never take yourself too seriously.

First become influenced, then try to become influential.

Spend more time listening than talking because you already know what you know.

Stay close to the fun.
· ·

When I say this is an opportunity to do well and then do good, you have to do well first and understand that in doing good, it may not be 700 jobs in some neighborhood— it may be five engineering jobs. But we could become, then, an engineering employer or location of choice. People, when they graduate from engineering school, for example, may say they want to go to ABC Co. because minorities advance in management, there is no glass ceiling, and they will have an opportunity of ownership after a certain number of years.

The things that create good solid corporate citizens take time. What we can do is provide a platform where people who are reflective of society are not prevented from excelling.

22

☀The Future

Edward E. Potter, *President, Employment Policy* *Foundation*

Edward E. Potter is president of the Employment Policy Foundation, a non-profit economic research foundation based in Washington, D.C. The group advises companies and executives on the future of the workforce and how to inspire entrepreneurial action and insight within an organization.

Question: Talk about business start-ups. Why are Americans so driven?

Answer: One of the keystones of the U.S. economy is what I call the entrepreneurial culture. In contrast to almost every other country in the world, you and I as individuals can take 15 minutes and have an incorporation. You don't need a lawyer, and so far, we have not placed a high penalty on company failure. A man or woman has a great idea. The idea flourishes for a while and then fails. We essentially don't create a stigma. The United States allows you to start fresh, to resolve your debts and move on.

· ·
CDs in the Changer

The Brandenburg Concertos by Bach

The Best of Thelonious Monk by Thelonious Monk

Feels Like Home and *Come Away With Me* by Norah Jones

Crash by The Dave Matthews Band
· ·

Eleven out of 100 people create a new business each year and to contrast that, in Germany, it's three out of 100 people. In the highest European Union country, it's four of 100 people. We're entrepreneurial in the sense that if we have an idea, we act upon it. It is partly our immigration heritage. People came to America to do better. Unlike Europe, we don't create a social safety net that makes people comfortable when they are laid off. We create some infrastructure, but because it is not a rich one, we create incentives for people to find another job or to start their own business.

Q: When you look at the early 21st century, you're looking at children of the 1980s, possibly the '70s, who are buying a house, maybe their second house, raising families, joining the workplace, starting a career—what are the expectations of that generation and how are those workers different from workers born in the 1940s, 1950s and 1960s?

A: They really are different. For one thing, there's polling that shows that Generation X-ers expect to retire earlier than Baby Boomers, which has all sorts of implications for our tight labor market. That's why this Social Security reform was pretty important. Boomers expect to work past 65. Another big difference is Generation X-ers expect to hold multiple jobs. Their view is that they are going to hold between 18 and 30 jobs before they're retired. Baby boomers expect to hold two, three or four, that is, we expected great job stability. The younger worker today doesn't expect the same job, same employer; the younger worker expects an ongoing skill improvement process.

They are not troubled by the prospect of working for an employer for six months and leaving if it doesn't work out. They are not uncomfortable with that. Keep in mind that this is essentially a country of small business.

Q: Why do you say that?

A: More than a majority of companies have 50 or less employees, so that's a lot of small businesses. Then the Fortune 500 account for 24 percent of the jobs. We have a huge number of self-employed people—about seven percent of the work force.

Q: What are some of the other trends you see happening in the workplace?

A: The first is the tight labor market and the issues of recruiting and retention of employees, and there's the need for workers to upgrade skills and for employers to want to train workers and create an environment where workers want to stay.

. . . .

BOOKS ON THE NIGHTSTAND

The Stone Raft by Jose Saramago

The Known World by Edward Jones

The Company of Strangers by Robert Wilson

. . . .

This is where immigration policy becomes very important. Half of all job growth in the United States in the 1990s was filled by immigrants. They filled two important niches. They work in the boiler rooms, doing the jobs that Americans no longer want to do, and that's a huge number of people. At the top end, they are fulfilling skill shortage needs.

We did a survey of 1,000 companies who are the biggest employers of skilled immigrants and found 34 percent of companies go where they need to go in the world to find the talent if they can't get it here.

• •
FAVORITE MEAL

Bacon cheeseburger, medium rare.
• •

Trend number two involves mergers, acquisitions and downsizings. In the past century, we've had seven waves of mergers and acquisitions. The current wave both in terms of quantity and dollar value is twice as big as any other point in our history.

That is not going to end. Built-in global competition means that, for businesses to compete, they are constantly going to be restructuring and adapting to new markets. You're already seeing that on one side the company is downsizing while on the other side they are upsizing. This is where Generation X-ers will do better. We Boomers don't do so well with keeping up with the pace of all that. How much energy do you want to expend on learning new skills, while knowing that, in reality, you just can't do it as fast?

Q: The merger curve—is it increasing in velocity or slowing?

A: The chart I can show you is going like this **[his arm shoots to the ceiling]**. We're talking about trillions of dollars that are being shuffled around. Policymakers respond to all this anxiety. I've not seen any surveys that compare and contrast anxiety between older and younger workers, but the big difference you see today is that where the anxiety was at the blue-collar level, beginning in the 1980s, white-collar workers are now affected as well.

The third trend is women in the workplace. Participation rates of married women are just as high as single women, just under 70 percent. We now have 42 percent of all families with dual earners in the work force. Over the last decade, this trend has leveled off but it creates stress on the amount of time that families have to deal with their own infrastructure. People have less time overall to take Johnny to baseball and Jane to ballet. There needs to be workplace flexibility. Employers need to come up with family-friendly policies, like telecommuting.

A '99 poll from Wirthlin Worldwide looked at employee-employer commitment. The questions are, "How committed are you to your employer?" and "How committed is your employer to you?" 65 percent said they are very committed but that they believed their employer was only committed to them at 35 percent.

If you ask the very same question of a person allowed to telecommute, 78 percent are very committed, and they believe their employer is committed to them at 56 percent. You've improved the relative relationships dramatically by just doing one thing.

23

✸A Shipshape Firm

Commander D. Michael Abrashoff, *US Navy*

The United States Navy is not exactly known as an incubator for free-thinking management strategies. But when Capt. D. Michael Abrashoff took over as commander of the U.S.S. Benfold, a $1 billion guided-missile destroyer, he decided to make the crew of 370 a human behavior laboratory. His mission: Encourage passion, commitment and peak performance.

Abrashoff, who has consulted for companies that include JP Morgan Chase & Co., Premier Healthcare Inc., Bank of America, Johnson Controls, Dow Chemical, and Federated Department Stores, is a graduate of the U.S. Naval Academy and former military assistant to former Secretary of Defense,

William J. Perry. He is the founder and chief executive of CEO Grassroots Leadership.

Question: You seem to be a fairly Generation X kind of guy in terms of your approach to people, their efforts and ambitions. That is, you're not afraid to bend or break rules. Should that kind of approach be encouraged at companies where the bottom line has immutable implications; take care of the bottom line or go belly-up?

Answer: If all we were to do is follow rules all the time, we'd need no mid-level managers. The CEO could write the regulation manual, and then you have the workers who could follow the manual. You need mid-level managers because not everything in the world is black and white. There are a lot of gray areas in business. That's why you need mid-level managers who are actively engaged and have the authority and empowerment to interpret the rules and regulations to fit the situations they face.

What we tried to do on Benfold was something to increase our bottom line. This was the only way I could figure out how to become a leader in our industry. At the end of the day, people became our competitive advantage in the relationships they created among themselves and our customers, whether U.S. taxpayers or the battle group commander.

· ·

CDs in the Changer

P.S.: A Toad Retrospective by Toad the Wet Sprocket

· ·

I always wanted to be the provider of choice. When you look at the other ships in the battle group, we all had the same capabilities, yet Benfold was the go-to-ship. It wasn't the technology. It wasn't the hardware. It was our people who were the competitive advantage. In business, a lot of companies offer the same product. The only way to get your customer to pay retail is to figure out your competitive advantage. I think it's how motivated and passionate your people are. You can feel that energy when you're dealing with workers who have that.

• •
BOOKS ON THE NIGHTSTAND

*Good to Great: Why Some Companies Make the Leap
...And Others Don't* by James C. Collins

*First In, Last Out: Leadership Lessons From the New York Fire
Department* by John Salka and Barret Neville

Plan of Attack by Bob Woodward
• •

Q: You write: "If we stop pinning labels on people and stop treating them as if they were stupid, they would perform better. Why not instead assume that everyone is inherently talented and spur them to live up to those expectations?"

You don't believe that, do you? How many times have you found that clerks could care less about you as a customer? In many cases, it's a systemic malaise—people just don't care.

A: Think about those few organizations where people do care. Take Southwest Airlines. That is not hype. It really is a great organization. It's not because they have different planes. At the end of the day, Southwest's competitive advantage is the people. It's statistically tougher to get a job at Southwest Airlines than it is to get into Harvard. There's one family where 11 of 13 members work at Southwest. That's the atmosphere that has been created by Herb Kelleher **[co-founder]**. He took a genuine interest in his employees, and they repaid him by providing a great customer experience for the fliers, and that's why Wall Street assigns such a high value to that company.

Q: How important is "management-by-wandering-about?"

A: Critical! On the Benfold, it was the most important part of my day, getting out and walking around. But you know, technology has not improved our communications ability within organizations. People think that if they write an e-mail or leave a voice mail, they're communicating. We are so stressed out we are losing the ability to communicate with fellow workers and our employees. I could have sat there and sent e-mails all day long on the ship, but what I did was make myself available as a leadership tool to my department heads.

If they had somebody who was working late on a project or somebody who did great work, in the morning when I met with my department heads, they would tell me, "Hey, this person worked until midnight. When you see him, give him a pat on the back." It was immediate. Within a day of their extra effort, they were hearing directly from me. I was looking them right in the eye and saying, "I sincerely appreciate the effort you put into this."

• •

DAILY PAPERS

The Washington Post

The New York Times

USA Today

The Wall Street Journal

• •

Compare that to getting an e-mail. There's no comparison. Sure, I had the advantage of having all 369 people within 505 feet of me. How do you do that when the sales force is spread out across the country or around the globe? That's the question I get asked all the time. I have to admit it's a challenge.

Q: Why don't executives do more of this?

A: It's because we're all stressed out. We're trying to do more with less. We're rushing around like maniacs. It's an easy thing to forget about, but to me praise is the one thing that pays the most important dividends. You can't order up great performance. Sure, you can threaten people, but they're going to do just the bare minimum to get by and not do one bit extra. Everything we did in Benfold was done to be the best.

24

❋Action

Andrea R. Nierenberg, *Queen of Networking*

Consultant and author Andrea R. Nierenberg, dubbed the "Queen of Networking" by *USA TODAY*, is an ardent advocate of the theory that businesses grow from quality contacts and people. Before a business can truly prosper, she believes, employees must embrace a culture of service, be empowered, and see supervisors as solution-oriented partners. Job enjoyment stems from attitude, and positive attitudes can not be purchased with a paycheck.

Among her blue-chip roster of clients are: *USA TODAY*, Chase Manhattan Bank, Columbia University, Estee Lauder, Meredith Corporation and AstraZeneca Pharmaceutical.

Question: Okay, say it's a month into the New Year, long enough to have broken personal resolutions, but anytime is a

good time for company resolutions. Any ideas?

Answer: Take the acronym *"ACTION." A* is for appreciation. Whether you are senior management or middle management, or whatever your job, show some appreciation to your employees.

In today's world, people are your most valuable property and commodity. If you want to retain your best people, show appreciation. One client said to me, "You know, that was such a good idea that I actually sent somebody a thank-you note. It's amazing how people will do more work for you."

C — Communicate. Everyone says we all communicate, but we really don't. Even though we might say we're listening, we really don't sometimes understand the other person. I make it a point to tell my clients to really listen to people who come into their office. Listen to people in meetings. We hear but we don't listen. It's like following that carpenter's rule: Measure twice but cut once. Really listen to people in your office or your meetings. You will avoid mistakes, and that will definitely go down to the bottom line.

T — Communicate more as a team. The whole team can play, as Babe Ruth said. Whether the whole team plays well is what it's about. In a lot of companies you have great individuals, but they don't play well together, so they're not worth a dime. Business is teamwork, but people don't know how to work in teams. Pay attention to co-workers and follow up. It's common sense. It's just not common practice.

• •

CDs in the Changer

Romanza **by Andrea Bocelli**

Paint the Sky with Stars **by Enya**

Lifescapes **by Pachelbel**

Mended **by Marc Anthony**

• •

Q: You always hear there is no "I" in team, but there isn't a paycheck in team, either. Most people get paychecks based upon individual initiative, individual accomplishments.

Why should any employee strive to work as part of a team?

A: You're right. But if everyone works on the same page, profits will increase. I read once when people go to a white-collar jail, they are seated around the table and told to work as a team. If one person screws up, everybody will go over across the street to the tougher prison where the people aren't as nice. All of a sudden people see the value of teamwork. Sure, we are paid based on our own measure and accomplishments, but the great employees inspire others to work together.

• •

BOOKS ON THE NIGHTSTAND

Listen Up, Leader by David Cottrell

The Connective Edge by Jean Lipman-Blumen

*Robert Crayhon's Nutrition Made Simple:
A Comprehensive Guide to the Latest Findings in
Optimal Nutrition*
by Robert Crayhon

• •

Q: Finish the word. What does "I" stand for?

A: *I* is for investing in yourself. The idea is to realize when you go into a meeting at a company somebody is going to be judging you. So look at how you present yourself. Look at your personal integrity. In the grocery store of life, what are you doing to enhance your brand image? What are you doing to make somebody pick you up off the shelf? You should work to come across as somebody who is constantly thinking about the good of the company.

O stands for opportunities. Look to start the year off fresh. The month off fresh, the week off fresh, the day off fresh. *O* can also stand for being organized. If everybody in the company were organized, they would be doing a service to themselves and to their fellow employees. We've all been in meetings that go on and on and on. Meetings could be shortened if people had an agenda and would be organized.

The final letter is *N* — network. And remember that the opposite of networking is notworking. Be accessible to everyone you meet. Increase your visibility and your circle of influence.

You don't just need to network when you need a job. You need a network to build alliances and connections and advocates throughout the company. Find ways to develop relationships up, down, sideways and across.

• •

ON THE COFFEE TABLE

Vogue, Fortune, Opportunity World,
Harvard Business Review, Lucky, Allure

• •

Q: Any other professional New Year's resolutions that could and should be made at all times of the year?

A: I think people need to write things down. When all is said and done, more is usually said than done. What I do is write things down. I make a commitment. Look at it this way. If you make a commitment, write it down. It's too vague otherwise. Be specific in your resolutions. But make your commitments smaller, something that's manageable. Remember—inch by inch, it's a cinch; yard by yard, it's hard.

25

❉Rethink or Sink

Neil Rackham, *Founder, President, Huthwaite, Inc.*

Neil Rackham has revamped sales forces at more than 30 companies. Born in England and reared in Borneo, Rackham returned to England before moving to America to become a consultant and author. He believes that sales organizations are undergoing dramatic changes as competition increases for a shrinking list of clients. Those changes are going to intensify as companies go global.

Question: In a lot of cases, salespeople talk about features of whatever they are offering. In today's world of business, is that a mistake?

Answer: It is a very serious mistake and it's one of those things that will put a salesperson out of a job. There are 18 million sales jobs in the United States and about 10 million of them are going away. The ones that are going away are the ones that you might call the "Talking Brochures." They are people who think it's their job to talk to potential customers about products.

• •

CDs in the Changer

Symphony No. 3 **by Philip Glass**

15th Symphony in A Major **by Dmitri Shostakovich**

• •

Basically, in the old days, you could make quite a good living with sales by telling people about your products. For instance, if you were a car salesman, unfortunate customers had to come to your wretched showroom and face the awful indignity of a miserable time because there was no other way they could learn about options on a car.

With the Internet and better sources of information, today the customer can go into the showroom knowing all the options, the factory invoice price, knowing more than the salesman knows. Anyone selling by talking about products is very inefficient and outdated. You can't afford to have salespeople who just do that. The salespeople who survive are the ones who do something different.

Q: Talk about the new buying reality and how customers have changed the way they make decisions.

A: What's happened is customers have moved in two separate directions. Some customers have moved to transactional selling. They see things as commodities. They don't care where they buy their next PC. As far as they are concerned, they are looking for the cheapest and quickest way to get the product. Those kinds of customers will buy cheap and easy. They go to the Internet. They will be prepared to buy over the telephone. They won't need the cost of face-to-face salespeople.

At the same time, other customers have moved in the

opposite direction. What they are asking for is more help, more depth, more expertise, salespeople who can solve problems for them. What they are buying is less the product and more the capability of creating value by solving a problem.

Q: How can you change a sales force? Old habits are strong, and they have obviously brought a measure of success.

A: Yes, and many salespeople probably won't be able to change. Thirty to forty percent of all sales forces are so dyed-in-the-wool, they're going to sell that way forever and will keep selling that way until they run out of opportunity; the lack of success will squeeze them out. For most salespeople, it's the manager who makes all the difference. A good sales supervisor and coach can encourage and really help people change. I've sorted out over 30 sales forces in my career and I know that when I look at a sales force and I want to know, "Can the sales force change?" It's not the salespeople I look at, it's the sales supervisors. They are the people who change a sales force.

Q: The question becomes, then, how do you change your sales supervisors?

A: The first thing you do: don't just promote good salespeople to become bad sales supervisors. Sales supervisors are managers, coaches, people who focus on how others perform. You recruit and develop a different kind of person, and your promotion strategy changes.

• •
BOOKS ON THE NIGHTSTAND

Personal History by Katharine Graham
• •

Q: Isn't there always going to be a need for a customer to seek loyalty? People want a branded and trusted relationship with someone who has provided service and materials.

A: There's truth to that, but it's equally true that the relationship itself is no longer enough. There are a lot of salespeople who used to build very good relationships and it used to bring them sales. Now we live in a time when customers say, "I like this salesperson a lot, but I buy from her competition because they're cheaper." Look at the loyalty, the relationship, the brand, as icing on the cake.

Brand is something that helps, but—in and of itself—it's not sufficient. Because products are all much more reliable these days, the brand isn't so important. For example, 10 years ago, the difference between the best and the worst cars on the market in terms of defects per 1,000 cars delivered was enormous. Today there's not much difference between a Mercedes and Hyundai in terms of defects. Customers expect that a product will perform, so they are less anxious about switching to a new product than they used to be.

26

☀Firm Debate

Patrick Lencioni, *President, The Table Group*

Patrick Lencioni has plenty of insight into executive team dynamics as president of The Table Group, a Lafayette, Calif., management consulting firm. Lencioni insists that the most important activities in a company happen around a table, where teams find clarity, achieve cohesion and develop strategies to excel.

Prior to founding The Table Group, which has a client list that includes Silicon Valley Bank, New York Life, FedEx Freight, VHA, Sam's Club, and Washington Mutual AON, Lencioni worked at the management-consulting firm Bain & Co., Oracle Corp. and Sybase, where he was Vice President of Organization Development.

Question: One of the premises of your approach has to do with team debate. Since when and where do members on any executive level team ever engage in unguarded debate? They almost never directly confront one another, do they?

Answer: It is extremely rare. And that's a tragedy because one of the greatest competitive advantages you can have is to have people who can quickly, nakedly cycle through issues and arrive at decisions because they don't hold anything back. And, as rare as it is, the companies that are best at it usually win. Intel and Microsoft are masters of conflict. People disagree with each other. They challenge one another's ideas. They do it without reservation and without being too particular with their words.

• •

CDs in the Changer

WOW 2004: Year's Top Christian Hits
by Various Artists

Shrek 2 Soundtrack **by Various Artists**

Brooks & Dunn's Greatest Hits **by Brooks and Dunn**

• •

There's no secret to why they are so good at responding to market needs and executing. Intel actually teaches classes in constructive conflict to employees because they don't want people to waste time in meetings, nodding their heads and smiling, and then walking out into the hallway and saying, "I think this is stupid." They want people to go to the meetings and say, "I think that's a dumb idea." General Electric was always pretty good at it. Jack Welch, the former chairman at GE, never hesitated to tell people what he thought, and he wanted his people to do the same thing.

Q: The down side to the lion's den is this—if you turn the lions loose on one another, aren't the lions going to get bloody? Aren't you going to turn some of your best people into walking-wounded after about six months of getting roughed up on a regular basis?

A: That's why trust needs to exist. If you have conflict without trust, then people use it to wound one another. Lack of trust is the first dysfunction. If you build trust on the team, then the conflict becomes constructive and productive, rather than destructive. That's the first order of business for any team—build trust. What I'm talking about when I refer to trust is the willingness to be vulnerable with one another, to admit mistakes and weaknesses but developing the confidence to know that that is not going to be used against you.

Trust is not intellectually predicting another person's behavior, it's the willingness to stick your neck out and say, "I'm sorry, I was wrong, I need help, I don't know the answer to this."

Q: You seem to be a big fan of mission statements, but not exactly the word "mission."

A: So many of those words become overused. One person's mission statement becomes another person's vision statement becomes another person's purpose statement. I almost think the vocabulary needs to be dropped and people need to describe it in words that actually mean something. Like, what is the reason we started our business? That's the core purpose. Why do we exist? Which behavioral traits will we not tolerate in the people we hire? That's the core value. What business are we in? What do we actually do? Those are the important questions.

. . . .
BOOKS ON THE NIGHTSTAND

The Bible

The Servant Leader by **Ken Blanchard**

The Foot Book by **Dr. Seuss**

Liar's Poker by **Michael Lewis**
. . . .

Q: One of your suggestions for insight into those values is to privately look at valued employees and hang adjectives on those employees. Then look at employees who have departed and hang adjectives on those people?

A: Yep! And then you take the list of the qualities of the first group and the qualities of the second group. Create another list of the executive team and see what's true about them. The confluence or overlap between the three lists is usually the fodder for your core values.

Q: These are fairly high-falutin' concepts if you own a hair salon, aren't they?

A: They are, but they don't need to be. The thing is, we are trying to encourage companies to answer the simple things about their business. Why did I start this business? What kind of people do we hire? Who do we compete against? How are we going to be different from the next guy or gal? What are we trying to accomplish right now? Who needs to do what for us to get there? That's why the vocabulary is so problematic. It shouldn't be high-falutin'. They should be basic questions that everybody in the company, whether you are the clerk or the stock boy or the CEO, can answer.

ON THE COFFEE TABLE

Sports Illustrated

What's crazy is when you have a little company of 10 people and not everybody can answer those questions, you're leaving goodness on the table. They all should be able to answer those questions.

Q: Clarity of purpose is extremely important, then.

A: Clarity means people don't have to go to their manager every time something has to be decided. If anything, that's the competitive advantage of a small company, too. A multi-national company may do so many different things, it's probably hard to get everybody on the same page. They are located all over the world. People talk about the nimbleness of a small company but they're really talking about getting everybody on the same page.

A friend of mine grew a company to $1 billion; he said if you can get all the people in a growing organization growing in the same direction, which is a big If, you can dominate any market against any competition at any time. It's hard to do, but smaller firms can do that. Then they can swim under the radar and out-maneuver the bigger ones who have a hard time getting everybody to come to work at the same time.

Q: In your best of all possible worlds, what is the salient point that people must mull over?

A: I think that one of the problems we have with business is either that we are overeducated or we are over-thinking things. Executives must find the courage to embrace simplicity and realize that success is about discipline and persistence more than it is about intellectual prowess. That is one of the keys to success. Too often we're looking for the silver bullet. As Andy Grove—the founder of Intel, of course—said the other day, business is hard. It's always been hard. It always will be hard. But it's not that complicated. It's not the smartest people in the world who succeed in business or leadership. It's the people who have the courage to look at things that matter and deal with them.

27

☀Delight

Dennis Speigel, *International Theme Park Services*

Dennis Speigel has no trouble tracing his career roots to the seed. It began when he was 13 and took a job working the gate to Coney Island Amusement Park in Cincinnati. He found he could count heads in the cars in line and figure out change five or six cars back from the car pulling up next to him. He stacked the change for each car on the counter so he could move people into the park at a swifter pace. Moving families into the park faster meant more money for the park.

Before long, Speigel had moved up through the ranks at Taft Broadcasting, which eventually bought Coney Island and created many major amusement parks in North America. By the time Speigel was 40, he left Taft to create his own amusement park consulting company, advising multinationals on whether to build or abandon plans for parks that cost upwards of $300 million.

Now a full-service amusement park design and operations firm, International Theme Park Services puts would-be owners in touch with investors, oversees construction, provides revenue projections and offers management expertise. In his career, Speigel has had almost every duty at an amusement park, from donning a cartoon character suit—Scooby-Doo—and walking the grounds to monitoring employee services to guarding the money at closing time. He has consulted on or developed amusement parks from Seoul to Makita, Manila, from Rio de Janiero to Beijing—in all, 300 projects in 36 countries. Through ITPS Speigel became a genuine Rollercoaster Tycoon. And he still sometimes climbs aboard for one more thrill ride.

Question: Tell me about that "crumb" of a contract falling off the Taft Broadcasting table so many years ago.

Answer: Well, 23 years ago I was Vice President of Development for Theme Parks at Taft Broadcasting. At that point in time, the industry was at its launch point internationally. There were very few theme parks around the world. Disney had just opened Tokyo, and it was an enormous success for the Oriental Land Co. Basically, they paid the park off in less than three years when normal pay-off is 15 years. This one was off the chart. Everybody in the world was watching it. The economy in the world at that time was very, very strong so companies were coming to us and asking us to participate in a project with them - as a consultant, as an investor, in any way they could possibly get us.

I had been out in the field working and managing the parks, so when I came back into the corporate office, I originally started doing the administration of the five or six parks we had at that time, and this became a large area of interest for Taft Broadcasting. I had a stack of proposed projects on my desk that was two feet high, and that's no kidding. These were basically requests for "How can you help us?" I had to go through them one by one and say this makes a lot of sense or this doesn't.

At that point in time, the theme park industry had not reached its zenith. They weren't realizing their greatest profits as yet. Our media division was out-performing our leisure division. So Taft's interest in theme parks in 1981-83 was a little on the wane. Guys wanted to pay us $250,000 to $400,000 to look at a project and just consult, but Taft execs remained cool to this business. I could see all these crumbs falling off the Taft table. To a mouse, a crumb is a pretty good chunk.

And at the same time, one of the companies that I had been working very diligently with in England came to me and said, "What we are really interested in is you, we want your fire in the belly. We want your knowledge of the industry." They asked me to come to work for them in some capacity.

I decided to take the big step, left all the stock options, all the perks that you get with a big company and I opened International Theme Park Services, and we stepped out into this project in England. Nothing came of it, actually. They kept the project alive for 12 years, but they couldn't get the final financing package. During that initial stage, it gave me a stepping stone to start ITPS, and I still talk to those guys. They are very good friends. In fact, the architect is world famous and we are now involved with him, years later, in another project.

We stepped out—boom, boom, boom, and the projects started coming to us from all over the world, from all the contacts we had made. We were very busy. I was going to move to England and take the one project on. But they couldn't get financing and we got terribly busy, so I couldn't leave.

Q: Ever have any nights driving home thinking to yourself, what have I done?

A: Yeah, still do. The industry is very slow right now, but that's okay. I'm in a different mode than I was 23 years ago. But we are still building and consulting. Here's an example: I'm on the phone with Pakistan this morning. We're talking to Beirut on Thursday. I heard from Qatar last night. But there have been many times when you ask, *Is it worth it?*

You're responsible for all these people, all their salaries, all their benefits, all their livelihoods and you have to be out there moving and thinking and ahead of the curve. This has been our company approach—when everybody was talking about the U.S., we went to Europe. By the time our competitors started heading to Europe, we went to Asia and locked up the biggest projects in Asia. By the time everybody figured out Asia, we went to South America and got all those projects.

Q: What has been the defining element that led you to shift focus from one corner of the globe to the other?
A: Where there's smoke, there's fire. One of the services we provide is the feasibility analysis work. Not many do that in the industry. We charge from $35,000 to $150,000 per study. So when we do a study, we get into it and determine if the thing is viable. What we were able to do, few companies were able to match, maybe two or three others in the world.

When we started, the industry was compartmentalized; a feasibility house, a design house, an operations management house. I had all those disciplines within one company. If I could get my foot in the door with the feasibility work and if the project was good, then I sold the design services and the operations management.

CDs in the Changer

Best of Broadway by Various Artists

The Very Best of Otis Redding by Otis Redding

Al Green's Greatest Hits by Al Green

The Very Best of Wilson Pickett by Wilson Pickett

Romances by Luis Miguel

As Time Goes By… The Great American Songbook Vols. I, II by Rod Stewart

Motown by Michael MacDonald

On any feasibility study, there shouldn't be any bias or conflict of interest, but because of our strong operating background, the other companies doing feasibility were theorists and we were practitioners. That's the way I sold ITPS. It built credibility because they knew we knew design and operations management. If they needed that done, they brought in ITPS.

Our business has allowed me to meet all the great barons of our time. For them, they all want to look at this industry because it's clean and they want to know a little something about it. When I traveled the world, I'd end up in the offices of some of the most powerful people in the world: Ruppert Murdoch, Donald J. Trump, Chou En-lai, people I otherwise would never know. I talked to the president of Pakistan this morning.

Now, we have a new concept, and it's the best I've seen in 25 years: "City of the Children" or "Kid City." We've identified big markets in the United States—Miami, New York, Atlanta, Los Angeles, Dallas, Chicago. But this concept overseas is going to be awesome.

Q: Talk about the scope and size of this industry. There are more trips to theme parks in the United States than all professional sporting events combined.

A: The industry in the U.S. did 280 million visits last year, give or take. What's the population of the U.S.? We got everybody, basically, at one time.

The 1960's were years of exploration. That's when the entrepreneurs like the Lamar Hunts and Bill Marriotts started looking at the industry to see if they could do what Disney did but on a lesser scale. The 1970s was a time of development. The 1980s was a period of maturation for the industry, figuring out how to really run them and make some money in a good economy. In the 1990s the old-line families were selling their parks off. Six Flags was starting to gobble them up. And now, in the millennium, we are seeing the globalization of the market. The top 50 parks are run by six groups. The industry now has reached a stall. There is saturation in North America and toward the end of the 1990s came worldwide saturations. All of the parks that could be built have been built.

Q: What about China?

A: China is different. I've been in China 20 years. That market is so different. Will there always be opportunity there? Well, yes. Disney will open its Hong Kong park this next year.

When that happens, it will pretty much take in all of southern China. I always tell people this: China is huge. I can name 10 cities in China, all of them over four million in population, and you'll know two of them. Chen Chen in the economic zone next to Hong Kong, when I started going there 20 years ago, it had 500,000 people. Today it has 7.5 million people.

Q: Most careers are exercises in serendipity. Yours has always been in the amusement park industry, starting at the gate at Coney Island.

A: My whole career has been in theme parks. I was 13 taking tickets and knew that's where I wanted to be when I was 58 and it's where I've been.

A while back, I figured out how far I've traveled. It's something like 22 times to the moon and back. It's true that it's better to be lucky than smart.

There has been some "right-place-right-time" going on with me. I was graduating from college when Taft was buying Coney. They needed to build a management team. I showed an interest. I came back to show them what I wanted to do, and how I wanted to be part of the business. I flew to parks on my own. I helped them set up the first recruiting program for young people. I went out and recruited at colleges for all the young people in the 1960s before anyone else did it. We were after young people, asked ourselves where are they and said, well, they're at high schools and colleges. So, during my spring break and on weekends, I'd go to colleges and set up a card table. I was the same age as the people I was recruiting.

I'd go to other parks to watch and learn. On a weekend, I'd go up to Cedar Point **[Sandusky, Ohio]** and watch them operate, see what they did. Talk about luck of the draw. My brother was learning to fly, an older brother. I said, "Let's fly up to Cedar Point." So we flew up there and when we got there that day, the management of Coney Island, all the senior guys were there walking around doing a tour. We ran into one another, and they saw me with a notebook, taking notes. It was like, "What the hell is he doing here?" That was a pretty good impression. They kept it in their minds, and I still have the memo in my office from Gary Wachs to me from 1969 when I was graduating from college. The senior guys wanted to get together with me to talk about my future, to talk about a job. That memo is framed.

Q: It's pretty audacious how far you've come from that little two-bedroom house where you grew up.

A: My career led me into certain paths. I capitalized on what I've done. As a consultant, I was paid by management to try to sneak into their parks. I've snuck into Disney World, Disneyland, and Universal Studios, in Florida and California. Sometimes I'd go and stand at the front gate and just watch for awhile and then tell them something that wasn't true to get in. I've rolled stamps across my hand, smeared ice cream on my hand to get past the handprint detector. You figure 200 people do something like that every day and well, *cha-ching,* you're losing big money.

• •

BOOKS ON NIGHTSTAND

My Life **by Bill Clinton**

—*"I think I pretty much know the ending."*

• •

I remember one night years ago at Paramount's *King's Island* before I had my own company. The armored car never showed up that night to pick up the money. I was in a backroom with another guy surrounded by that day's take. It was over $1 million in small bills stacked all around the room. For a moment, he and I looked at each other and we both had the same thought— *Take the money and go.* Then we went, "Nah, no way."

I've done everything at an amusement park. Once, I was hired to dress up as Scooby-Doo to check up on workers. That was tough duty. What people don't know is the tail is connected with this device that goes through your legs like a jockstrap. So a 4-year-old pulls on the tail—*Hello!* And it's hot in that suit. I was dying in it and not getting much done, as I recall. But one of the first rules is no matter what, you don't take off the head. On that dash to the dressing room, I was just wading through kids—*Get out of my way!* Now I'm getting toward the end of my career. I have flown six million miles. I've traveled to 40 countries and I've seen changes sweep through the industry.

When I was president of our industry trade association, it was a very xenophobic industry at the time. While we were called the International Association of Amusement Parks and Attractions, we were really a domestic group. When I went into that position, well, I had been on the board of directors of the association for maybe seven years, I decided that if we were truly going to be an international association, we had to reach out. I brought in the Germans, the Russians, the Brazilians and the Japanese. I almost doubled the size of the membership. I understood the international markets, the international arena, and I wasn't afraid of them.

At one point, I nominated myself chairman of the education committee, looked at three or four universities and, since the obvious one was Cornell, I went there and asked if they'd be interested in a program on amusement park operations for their hotel management school. I wrote the glossary and the syllabus for the course. At the time, I was talking to Oxford, England, and Hong Kong Polytech. Cornell wanted it bad.

Fourteen years later it's still going strong. There is tremendous international involvement. People come for ten days and participate in a course of Theme Park 101—case studies, marketing, operations, all facets.

Q: Taller, faster, longer coasters. Have coasters finally hit the wall of what's possible?

A: No, the technology today can now stretch what the body can stand. We can do almost anything from a design standpoint. You'll see a 1,000-foot coaster within the next ten years. I remember when we weren't at 200 feet, and I said you'll see a 400-foot coaster. Well, we're already above that. From a technology standpoint, there's no question about it. It's going to happen, but the body can only take so much. For me, personally, I think we're at a point where we need to focus on the entertainment aspect of it instead of the speed and thrill.

Q: Aren't amusement parks, ultimately, about creating memories? Family memories, family moments?

A: That's true, but, honestly, our industry has hit a wall.

We're at a point now where not only has growth in development come to a halt but the growth in attendance has come to a halt. We've hit a pricing wall. I had a friend call me this week. He took his grandkids to *King's Island*. He's 66 years old, and that trip cost him $1,700. He bought the tickets, went in and let them do anything they wanted. A ring toss is five bucks now. When we opened *King's Island*, it was 50 cents. I mean, it's expensive. So when I say the industry has hit the wall, it has. Costs are up, profits are down.

What really changed the industry was the season pass. It can virtually be bought for the price of one-and-a-half visits. There has been a dilution. From an admissions standpoint, they're pretty much giving the tickets away. The market controls the discounting rather than the park.

If you look at the industry as a whole, a park in the Midwest will do about three million, maybe 3.3 million in attendance and, in less than 130 days, that's a helluva lot of people. When I worked there and managed it, we did attendance by ticket type. That is, we segmented it—full fare or a la carte, promotional discounts, and group sales like churches and organizations. Back then, the a la carte was 37 percent of our business. Know what it is today? Two percent or less.

• •

FAVORITE MEAL

"Anything cooked by Chef Jean-Robert de Cavel, owner of Jean-Robert at Pigall's. But my favorite meal is my mother's fried chicken, potato salad, baked beans, deviled eggs, and strawberry shortcake for dessert."

• •

Q: The manifestation of fun, does it change from culture to culture? And how does waiting in line or experiencing a ride differ from culture to culture?

A: Well, for example, in Singapore, people are very timid. They don't like extreme thrills on a roller coaster, which is what Americans like. They're tied to their mother's apron strings a much longer time. In certain emerging markets, you don't need to be as sophisticated because they haven't been through step one, two and three, that is, a coaster that turns you upside down nine times. In Asia, Korea, Japan, after World War II, they had to work their asses off to rebuild, so they were 15 to 20 years behind America on having leisure time. However, that is changing because of the Web. People see what's out there now, so the levels of sophistication internationally are coming up.

The basic common denominator in our industry all over the world is fun—everybody wants to have fun. Your level of fun might be a little different than mine, but we all want to have fun.

Now the Chinese will get on a roller-coaster with two loops or four loops, and they'll sit there and, while they're riding, they'll never make a noise. Never scream. Never make a face. They do the loops. No scream. Nothing. Not one noise through the loops. And as soon as they get off the ride, it's *WHAAAAAEEEEEE.*

The most fun though, at amusement parks, are the Americans, Mexicans and Brazilians. It's just about the attitude toward having fun. Honestly, I'm not sure that the Brazilians don't have more fun than everybody else.

People waiting in line in Brazil have the greatest time waiting in line of any group I've ever met in my life. They can wait five minutes or two hours, and they sing and dance the entire time. They applaud. They sing. They dance. They wiggle. They have more fun than any group of people on the planet. My standard line with Brazil is that if I'd gone there when I was 25, I would have never come back. But I would have been dead by the time I was 27. I would have been partied out. They are the greatest.

28

☀Research

Doug Hall, *Eureka! Institute*

When marketing guru Doug Hall of Eureka! Institute looks out across the business landscape of America, he can't help but dwell on a staggering statistic. For every new business that makes it, three others struggle and fail.

After a successful career as a business and new product developer at P&G, Hall broke away to create a company that surveyed and projected consumer acceptance of new retail products. His funding? Three VISA cards. His location? The basement of his house.

His Richard Saunders International, which was Ben Franklin's pen name, evolved into Eureka!Ranch and then Eureka!Inventing, where a diverse array of companies like

AT&T, PepsiCo and Nike come to invent new products or develop new business strategies.

Thousands of innovative sessions, six years and $20 million led to the creation of Merwyn Technology, a quantitative concept computerized advisor that forecasts strategy for products and ideas. Merwyn compares written ideas for a product with consumer data points from about 10,000 other products on the market and offers an analysis of the likelihood of the product being viable during the next five years. Corporate clients use Merwyn as a replacement for concept refinement focus groups. Merwyn is accurate to within one to two percentage points of predicting actual market acceptance of 900 products, five years after those products were introduced.

Hall is also the author of several business books, including *Jump Start Your Brain* (Warner Books), *Meaningful Marketing* (Emmis Books) and *Jump Start Your Business Brain* (Betterway Books).

Question: So, when people walk through grocery stores is there a continuous loop playing in their heads of Overt Benefit, Reason to Believe, Dramatic Difference, Overt Benefit, Reason to Believe...

Answer: People are thinking, "I have a problem, I need solutions." The more common questions are: *What's in it for me? Why should I believe you? Why is this product any different from anything else that's out there*?

To start with the really big picture, our Merwyn is a dramatic change from where we've been in the past. We are major league number gronks. Over the last six years, with this research, we've gone from being barefoot gurus to becoming more like stat wizards. It's about playing probabilities. All of this research is about defining how to increase your odds of success. My training is in chemical engineering, and the old chemical engineer in me has had a field day with analyzing stuff and understanding the strategies that give companies and people a better chance at success.

We can play slot machines, or we can play blackjack. What we offer customers is the option to play blackjack instead of slot machines. It increases the odds for companies to win more, lose less, and make more money. That's the exciting news. Business success isn't random. There are reproducible laws that, when followed, should dramatically increase your odds of success. This isn't technology for the sake of technology. It's mind-boggling what this system can do.

CD IN THE CHANGER

College of Piping Celtic Festival

Q: Are you the contrarian at this point, that when a nation is in an economic lockdown, that that's when it's time for a company to cut loose with the reins on spending?

A: People have finally decided that they can't do it with smoke and mirrors. When you have advanced technology like Merwyn, you can see into the future. You can quantify. Instead of just some guru preaching to you, Merwyn is statistical analysis based on facts. This has a lot of appeal to people. Clients are turning around and saying, "Hey, this is what I really need—a real tool, not just somebody's opinion, but data."

They're saying, "Guess what, I'm not going to gamble my job on someone's opinion. I want the numbers." That's where things are going. I will never tell you that you will succeed and I will never tell you that you will fail and anybody who does is lying. Other than God almighty, nobody knows anything for certain. Out of 10,000 ideas, we've only had one that looks like it will score above 90 percent probability of success, and you can't get below 10 percent on the Merwyn rating. The fact of the matter is, most stuff fails. You have better odds with a Las Vegas slot machine than you do with the average new product or service.

Q: You contend that 75 percent of the new businesses out there fail within five years. That's a pretty astounding number.

A: Research shows that it can get as high as 90 percent failure for venture investors. Venture people are some of the dumbest investors I've ever found. Their track record is just dismal. Most are just plunderers—a fancy pyramid scheme. What they do is take the company, dress it up and flip it [sell it] so they can get their money out. They don't actually run a business or stay with a business. Their job is to flip it to somebody down the food chain. They aren't really businesspeople.

Q: Companies don't make it then, as I understand it, mostly because people just get tired.

A: The reality is that it's just too much work—97 percent of businesses have less than $1 million in sales. They're the people who really grow businesses. One hundred percent of the new jobs are coming from small businesses. Corporations are just getting smaller. Most small businesses give up, not because of debt, but because it's just not worth the effort.

There's nothing sadder in my mind than a business person having a dream, starting their own business, and then giving it up because it's not worth the effort. What we found was you can literally double your odds of success by doing some basic things combined with use of advanced tools like Merwyn.

You have to offer your customers an overt benefit, do what you say you're going to do, and then make sure you're dramatically different. If you are not dramatically different, you're a commodity and you sell for commodity prices and before long commodity pricing means you're not making any profits, and it's the path to ruin.

• •
BOOKS ON THE NIGHTSTAND

The Deming Management Method
by Mary Walton and W. Edwards Deming

Five Equations that Changed the World
—The Power and Poetry of Mathematics
by Michale Guillen, Ph.D.
• •

Q: You've done a lot of public speaking and writing, in addition to new product development. Writing is such a painful process that most people avoid it whenever possible. Is it something you avoid, too?

A: Yeah, it is. Somebody once said that you write these books and then at the end, you find out what you were really talking about. There are three things I can see when I sit back and wonder, *What did I learn from this?*

. . . .

BOOKMARKS

www.cbc.ca

(Canadian Broadcasting Corporation)

. . . .

The first is that writing is non-negotiable. If you can't say it in words, you will never get other people to buy into the vision. You've got to be able to articulate it. If you can't do it, you need to find somebody who can. Merwyn requires you to do that. You've got to get it in writing. Yes, it's hard and painful, but failing is more painful. You need to tell your story from the perspective of the customer, not you the seller.

Business success isn't random. The opportunity is for improvement of a message to attract customers and then convert that attraction into closed sales. A lot of people have given up. I'm here to say you can win. You can succeed.

29

☀Mission

Frances Hesselbein, *Former CEO, Girl Scouts of America & winner of the Presidential Medal of Freedom*

Frances Hesselbein, a winner of the Presidential Medal of Freedom from President Clinton, has had first-hand experience with the best practices of nonprofit management. At the ceremony, President Clinton pointed out a character trait that has long marked Hesselbein's approach: "Since Mrs. Hesselbein forbids the use of hierarchical words like 'up' and 'down' when she's around, I will call this pioneer for women, volunteerism, diversity, and opportunity, not 'up,' but 'forward,' to be recognized."

A former Girl Scout troop leader, Hesselbein rose to become Chief Executive Officer of Girl Scouts of the USA. Today she is Chairman of the Board of Governors of Leader to

Leader, formerly the Peter F. Drucker Foundation for Nonprofit Management.

Question: What can private companies learn from nonprofits and the challenges that nonprofits have met and overcome?

Answer: Peter Drucker has written extensively on this. He says there are three great lessons business can learn from nonprofits. One is the effectiveness of a board of directors; number two is the power of mission; number three is the ability to mobilize and engage knowledge-workers the way nonprofits mobilize and engage volunteers.

Q: Which of those is the most important?

A: I think you would begin with mission. This is true in all sectors. We mobilize people around a mission because mission is why we do what we do. It's the reason for being. The most successful organization has a short, powerful and compelling mission statement that they hold before their people as the sole reason that organization exists. When you are mission-focused, the power of the mission builds and becomes a very potent force in building a cohesive and successful organization.

Q: A challenge for all companies is to find a committed, experienced and loyal work force. In recent years, the companies that marry their philanthropy with their work force have an appeal to the X and Y generations that is compelling to those workers. Is that a fair assessment?

A: Yes. It's fair and can be measured and demonstrated. Peter Drucker has a wonderful quote: When you have people in business who then move into the social sector or are engaged by having their own people as part of an initiative with a nonprofit, then that company and those people have moved from success to significance.

Q: Moved from success to significance... that's a nice phrase.

A: Yes, don't you love that? You see, whatever you want to call those generations, people today are looking for significance in their lives. They want significance and meaning beyond a paycheck. And one of the most valuable and powerful ways to provide this, I believe, is in these remarkable partnerships, alliances, and collaborations where a nonprofit identifies a critical need in a community, creates a partnership with a corporation and, together, the critical need is addressed.

It's not the old, "I write checks, you do the work." It is the people of the corporation and the nonprofit in partnership finding significance and satisfaction. They share a vision. They share a commitment, and they share the satisfaction of being able to change lives.

The 1.5 million nonprofit organizations in this country have a common bottom line—changing lives. When we do this, we build community. This is a great adventure for many people in corporations who feel it's their responsibility to move beyond the walls and partner with a nonprofit organization so they can address a particular community need.

Q: Say you have a hardware store. They have a small payroll. How can that company find a nonprofit or a mission that will be compelling and appealing to the people who take home the paycheck each week?

A: It is not only the hardware store finding a nonprofit. It's how does a nonprofit move out and say, "This is what we do. We are meeting a need and we need your partnership." Maybe that hardware store has a resource they can provide or people who can be part of a marvelous joint team. It is amazing. Size is not the deciding factor of success. It is shared commitment, shared resources, and shared energy.

Q: There's going to be more than one hard-boiled executive out there who's going to read this and say, "Awwww, it's just another thing to eat at my margins—take away my bottom line. We're facing rising advertising costs and swooning revenues, I can't afford this."

A: He is also losing his best and brightest people, perhaps. One of the ways you keep a committed and energetic work force is to provide something beyond the paycheck.

Q: What is it about the human condition—about how some people are hard-wired to do good?

A: I think it is part of the heart and spirit of the American people. It's our tradition since the early days of the country for people to help people. It's part of the culture of our country. It's part of the greatness of our country.

30

❋Work by Design

Stephen C. Schlegel, *Hixson Associates*

Hixson Associates, an architecture, engineering and interior design firm, surveyed 657 Fortune 1000 and dot-com business managers and found that three of four respondents gave their office space an average grade, with most managers believing that their existing offices hurt productivity. Hixson's research also revealed that telecommuting and the mobile work force are expected to triple over the next five years. About 50 percent of the work force will be telecommuting, with the average worker spending just 36 percent of his time in the work space, says Stephen C. Schlegel, a former Hixson executive who is currently Chief Executive and President of the International Association of Food Industry Providers.

Question: What was the most significant finding in the Hixson survey?

Answer: That knowledge-workers believe they could increase productivity significantly with more compatible work environments. What it amounts to is they're working in an environment that doesn't support their work processes. Technology has enabled these knowledge workers, both outside and inside, to do a heck of a lot more by giving them access to more knowledge than ever before. They want to be more creative. There's more participation/teaming and the facility frustration means not all the tools are there when they need them. For example, how many times do people need to find a conference room or team center and can't? That's a universal issue.

• •

CDs in the Changer

Straight No Chaser,
an Indiana University a Cappella Men's Singing Group

and

"A variety of Windham Hill offerings."

• •

Q: Teaming takes space and space carries a per-square-foot price tag. How can companies provide those opportunities without hammering the bottom line?

A: First and foremost, you have to build a business case. There is a business case that is applicable to the office environment that addresses above-line issues like growth and productivity and attracting and retaining key knowledge workers. Yes, there are also real estate costs, operating costs, and maintenance costs to control and maintain. You have to build a case based upon understanding the work processes of the business unit or team. You have to understand the needs for technology and to integrate technology with the facility and human resources requirements. In other words, our survey of knowledge workers said, align facilities to my work processes, give me the tools and, I'm telling you, I can increase productivity by 30 percent or more.

Q: The Hixson survey found that six of ten senior managers would give up a portion of a bonus for better work space for people they manage. Do you believe that's true?

A: I believe these knowledge workers are telling us they are committed to investing in the immediate and near-term growth of the business and that's where their rewards would be. It's a return on investment that knowledge workers are applying in their own mind; they are willing to invest in the company and, if results grow 30 percent, they'll share in that. It was an open-ended question and we did not lead the respondents in any way, shape or form. Actually, 10 percent of senior managers said they would reinvest their entire bonus back into work space redesign if that would support their efforts.

Q: How else is workplace configuration important?

A: It will allow your company to attract and retain top knowledge workers. To quote Winston Churchill, "Once we shape our buildings, thereafter they shape us." As far as employee attraction and retention, which is a huge issue that we are all dealing with, the survey points out that you need to provide a productive work environment so knowledge workers can contribute in an environment that energizes them and supports their work process.

Q: The findings suggest that companies will see increased telecommuting and less employee time in a defined workplace. Why then should companies spend money on a workplace that will see fewer and fewer people in the years to come?

A: The issue as it relates to telecommuting is that there will be a huge rate of growth in the next three to five years, far outdistancing what any of us expected. Our national survey [many] years ago, of Fortune 100 chief executives, projected that by the year 2000, about 20 percent of the work force will be non-territorial with no designated workspace that an individual can call their own. This recent survey validated that finding. What is astounding is the velocity of the rate of growth of telecommuting of the non-territorial knowledge worker. But those workers will still need to collaborate, handle specific tasks in-office, get caught up on company news, and do some business in the office.

Q: Can you break out what percentage of the work force will be office-bound?

A: This survey identified that only 16 percent of this mobile work force will be in the office 10 percent of the time or less. The other 84 percent of that work force will be coming into the office at rates exceeding that, between 10 percent to 30 percent for one large group, and between 30 percent and 60 percent for the rest.

• •

BOOKS ON THE NIGHTSTAND

Good to Great: Why Some Companies Make the Leap and Others Don't **by Jim Collins**

Zagat America's Top Golf Courses

The Worst-Case Scenario Survival Handbook for Golf **by Joshua Piven, James Grace, Brenda Brown**

Jump-Start Your Business Brain **by Doug Hall**

The Five People You Meet in Heaven **by Mitch Albom**

Battle Ready **by Tom Clancy.**

• •

Q: Are there emotional concerns between the mobile and non-mobile segments?

A: One concern is a fear of alienation. If workers are out too much, the question is will the worker really feel like a part of the company. The other side is the resident knowledge worker with a permanent office address - you have this influx of people coming in, so how do they interact with the mobile group? It's a huge cultural issue. There could be envy of the sense of freedom of the mobile work force. From the management standpoint, the question becomes: how do I lead these people? How do I supervise them?

Q: How do you figure out what a company will look like in the future and therefore, what kind of space needs it

will have?

A: One size does not fit all. As we go forward towards the office of the future, it's imperative to understand cultural issues—the work processes of resident and mobile workers, the management issues and technology. We must create a space that is flexible enough to meet today's unique needs and that is able to evolve with enterprises. For some clients, the best solution is private offices for their unique concentration zone areas and collaboration zones where people can get together. For others, there are unique kinds of zones where they need to engage with customers directly, and that's another client concern. The office of the future is about mass customization.

Q: Wait a minute, isn't that oxymoronic? Mass customization?

A: What I mean is you have to find elements that are mass-produced and have the creativity to customize those standard items to support work process and knowledge workers. For one of our dot-com clients in Silicon Valley, they don't know how fast they are going to grow. The growth has been so dramatic that flexibility is paramount. They have to create an environment to attract top talent. It's a real trick.

You'd be surprised at how forward-thinking companies are being placed into facilities with last-century standards, environments that just don't fit the way these companies want and need to work.

• •
FAVORITE MEAL

Grilled Copper River Salmon with asparagus and portabella mushrooms.

• •

31

✳Family

Ellen Frankenberg, PhD., *Frankenberg Group*

Author and psychologist Ellen Frankenberg has been consulting families in business for ten years as chief executive of the Frankenberg Group. Her firm evolved from a family psychological consulting practice she created in the 1980s. She sees emerging women-led businesses as a vital force in American commerce.

Question: What led you to make the transition from family psychologist to family business consulting?
Answer: I had a number of clients who would come to me with typical family issues—facing a divorce or maybe an adolescent on drugs—and, as I met with them, I realized that

often there was a family business at risk. Gradually, I began to work with more and more of those families as they sorted out decisions that affected not only families but the continuity of their businesses. The issues are often the same—communications skill and conflict resolution.

. . . .

CDs in the Changer

Adagio for Strings by Samuel Barber

The Look of Love by Diana Krall

Come Away with Me by Norah Jones

. . . .

Q: What can be helpful from the field of family psychology for companies?

A: There are a lot of helpful concepts from family psychology that busy entrepreneurs haven't taken the time to think much about. For instance, the first premise of communication is that the shortest distance between two points is a straight line. If you think about the implications of that for a family business, relationships can become entangled, especially if a family mixes business decisions with family concerns. Decisions made from a business perspective have to be based on data, the competency needs of the marketplace, responsibilities to customers, the supplier, the IRS, etc. There is accountability.

Within the family context, you are thinking in emotional terms. You may be thinking about what's best for your son because you love him and want to follow a tradition of passing the business onto the son. That's where families get into most major problems. There can be emotional spaghetti that people need to think about.

Q: Presumably some of the 37 percent of the companies in the United States that are headed by women are also headed by mothers. What are the implications of a growing number of businesses being run by women? What are the implications for America's daughters?

A: Businesses led by women contribute $2.28 trillion to the economy and employ 25 percent of all U.S. workers. Although family businesses are still male-dominated, there are more women in top executive positions in family firms than in other firms. Biology will always be destiny. The life span of women will be significant. At the turn of the century, women had a life span of 42 years, now it has doubled to 80-something in the U.S. And there's more and more research that male and female brains do differ in how they process events and experiences. The classic example is that women ask for directions and men find their own way. The point is that in cyberspace, it doesn't matter how tall you are. Business today doesn't require a lot of heavy lifting, and the crucial business tool of our time, the computer, is sexless.

• •

BOOKS ON THE NIGHTSTAND

Crossing the Unknown Sea: The Pilgrimage Between Work and Identity **by David Whyte.**

— *"A remarkably well-written story of one man's journey from corporate America to the life of a poet."*

• •

Q: Are women better suited to be business leaders of the future?

A: Family firms today can capitalize on the female advantage—the "advantage" is based on Sally Helgesen's research, which is presented in her book *The Female Advantage*. She shows that women will adopt more flexible solutions. That they're going to integrate work with the rest of life. They'll take time in the middle of the day to call a daughter to be sure she got home OK from school. Women develop teams in which information is shared instead of hoarded competitively. Their leadership is probably going to work from the center like a web, rather than like a ladder, with power focused only at the top.

Q: Like a spider, eh?

A: I suppose. They'll move back and forth from the center but they will be more inclusive. Women build teams, but also change teams and are less likely to embrace rigid titles as the basis for authority. They'll tolerate interruptions much more readily. Women nurture.

Women develop their female identity by bonding and connecting with their mother. Boys develop their masculine identity by separating and differentiating from their mother. So guess what? Women, as a rule, think first of the impact on the other before they make decisions. Males generally think first of their own personal goals—shooting par on a Saturday afternoon. Also, men have been given much more freedom from mothers and fathers to pursue their own goals. They don't have to be protected.

Women's leadership can bring more customer-focused solutions and less ego. It leads to just-in-time delivery. It leads to collaborative team-building. Women are usually thinking first of impact on others, and that's why they're doing laundry at midnight. They are worried that their kid is not going to have a clean shirt for soccer the next day. This has tremendous implications for the way they run their business. They are not just thinking of their own agenda.

Q: What should mothers be telling their daughters about careers?

A: If you want to prepare your daughter to be a Chief Executive Officer, the messages you give will be extremely powerful. Let her know she is loved and special, that she is unique and can do anything she wants—she can be an astronaut, she can go to Harvard, she can take risks, take a canoe over the rapids, she can introduce herself to the new kid, she can try out for a sport. Simply, she is entitled to dream of greatness. If a woman wants to get to the top of a major corporation, usually they do it a different way, through inclusion rather than exclusion. They build collaborative relationships rather than competitive relationships.

32

☀Prejudgments

Gladys Gossett Hankins, Ph.D, *Telvic*

Gladys Gossett Hankins, Ph.D., thinks racial and gender stereotypes and prejudices—sometimes conscious and other times subconscious—play a far greater role in our workplaces than people realize. From Hungary to China, Lebanon to Japan, Brazil to Russia, Gosset Hankins has taught executive, manager and worker strategies to bridge gaps. She is a former Senior Manager of Minority Business Development for the Procter & Gamble Co.

Question: Somewhere out there is a sixth-grade boy, and he's white. He's getting A's and he goes to college, graduates

and applies for his first job at a multinational company. So he's sitting across from a human resources executive who gets a bonus if he hires a minority.

Can you look that sixth-grader in the eye today and tell him that when he goes for that first job interview, he will be judged by his ability and not by the color of his skin?

Answer: Well, definitely that would be a case where he is being judged by the color of his skin.

I think, early on, companies made a lot of mistakes. They were hurrying up and trying to comply with affirmative-action legislation and put a lot of people in a lot of positions without examining whether or not it was the right thing to do. As we have become a little more sophisticated, the pressure is off because so much has changed as far as the numbers go. We went from zero to comfortable numbers [of women and minority men in the work force], so now there is less pressure to "put a body here." Besides, if I just "put a body here" it's a reflection on me if I continue to put people into positions and they fail.

All things being equal, if I have to choose between a white boy or a woman of whatever race—who both worked hard to achieve—and my records show that I need to bring more women in, I'd hire the woman. I don't know how to speak to the impact of that on that particular person, the white boy.

It seems as though when we hire or promote a woman or a minority male, it's blown way out of context. It seems to some as though the company is shifting—like, *"They're* taking over. *You have to be careful now"* —they' being women and minorities.

One black man gets a job and 50 white men say, "That should have been my job." Every one feels put upon. Why? Because they assume this person got the job even though he or she was less qualified than they are. It's that assumption of "less-qualified" that draws from stereotypical beliefs and expectations that we grow up with. The question of whether or not someone is less qualified is almost always raised when the individual is from a group other than a white male. But when one white male is hired over another, it's never a question.

Q: Why are race, gender, prejudice and discrimination such a pervasive issue—that 140 years after the Civil War you

still hear men on downtown streets shouting names at women who are just walking home from work?

A: I've tried to analyze that because beliefs and stereotypes are so deeply ingrained and yet they are learned. They are not natural in our genes. We are not born with those stereotypes. We learn them. And many times, those stereotypes are taught at such an early age, when we are shaping our values and beliefs, that we do not recall them.

The media is one of the major shapers of ideology, beliefs and values. Even if it seems innocent, like a television program, it is sending stereotypical messages. For many years, for adults, for people my age, television programs did not represent different races.

· ·

CDs in the Changer

If I Had My Way by Nancy Wilson

Music to Disappear In by Raphael

Soulful by Reuben Studdard

The Icon is Love by Barry White

Grace by Kathleen Battle

· ·

In that absence there is a message: insignificance. In a wonderful book from the late 1950s called *The Nature of Prejudice,* one of the all-time best books on the topic, there was a study of 100 movies. Of those movies, only 12 had blacks in them playing something other than disparaging roles—the shuffler or maid or someone who was the object of ridicule. It was programmed into peoples' minds. Our values are shaped without us often even thinking about it.

In Iowa, there was a study of children in the third grade that was so poignant to me. Following the death of Martin Luther King, children who had not ever seen a black person in real life, even at the age of eight, spewed out hate. Where had they learned that?

Q: There are probably few examples of overt racism

and prejudice in the workplace today because individuals who harbor those feelings and sentiments do a pretty good job of repressing them, if only for fear of a lawsuit or federal action. It is your contention that there are subtle and under-the-surface prejudicial currents in most organizations and workplaces? How do you know?

A: There are patterns that show that both women across all races and minority men tend to have higher attrition rates for reasons that seem innocuous. For instance, leaving to pursue other interests, or you will see lower promotion rates.

The confidentiality of wages, for example, enables a system of favoritism. Because you don't get to know what I am paid, somebody can be on the low end of the range and stay there, because their supervisor doesn't like them, and be none the wiser.

Time and time again, women will be in a meeting. They will make a statement and be totally ignored, but when Fred makes the point, it's the greatest thing since sliced bread. These are patterns that say, "Something is wrong with this picture."

· ·

BOOKS ON THE NIGHTSTAND

Madam Secretary, A Memoir by **Madeleine Albright**

Long Walk to Freedom: The Autobiography of Nelson Mandela

The Key to Rebecca by **Ken Follett**

Four Blind Mice by **James Patterson**

The Selected Poems of Nikki Giovanni

· ·

I've done dozens of workshops since the late 1970s in Canada, the United States, Europe, Japan and Latin America. These workshops show very little difference in stereotypes, whether the year was 1978 or 1998. It's not at a conscious level, and the stereotypes come from groups in separate rooms. We'll have mixed groups doing a stereotype list about women, and there is a preponderance of negative stereotypes; women are weak, sissies, manipulative, catty, and we hear it over and over and over. And it's always the same.

The ones about men tend to be less hurtful. There are some negatives but mostly positive. And then the interesting thing is when every group agrees to the ten prevalent stereotypes in the workplace—stereotypes about women, about men, about blacks and about whites, without exception the ten prevalent stereotypes about women will be negative. Maybe on occasion it's nine to one, nine negative and one positive, but without exception, the stereotypes about men are ten positives. For blacks, it's ten negatives—everything from *welfare* to *dumb,* to *lazy,* to *can't make decisions.*

When people generate this list, they think it's just too ridiculous, until they come together and review it, and all of a sudden they realize, in the workplace, a person will automatically be credited with having these negative qualities; they are going to have to live with them for the rest of their adult work lives, and it happens as soon as they walk in the door.

Q: Many companies put mentoring systems into place to find the articulate achievers, the would-be senior managers. Does mentoring ever work against a person?

A: Mentoring can be helpful or of no help, but it is unlikely that it will be hurtful. I've heard a white male say how it was helpful. The mentor always looked out for him so his name was thrown into a hat for the best assignments.

· ·
ON THE COFFEE TABLE

O—The Oprah Magazine,

Ebony, Town and Country,

and

Essence.
· ·

Typically, mentors at the higher levels are men because women haven't gotten there yet—though they are getting there slowly. So a man may try to develop a mentor relationship, and men are just more comfortable with other men. There are gender things that happen between a male and a woman, sexual connotations or fears. A man may think, if I invite Alice to lunch, people may start talking. I don't need it and she doesn't need it.

As a male mentor, one may feel more confined mentoring a woman. If I go for a beer or play golf or sit with coffee for a long period of time, I can do that with Bill, but it just doesn't look right if I do that with Alice. Truly, if I am mentoring these people and have grown up with my own set of stereotypes, well, when do those stereotypes ever leave me? Clearly, I am going to lend some favoritism to Bill. He looks like me. We golf together. I'm a white man. He's a white man. But Alice, I don't want to put her in a situation where she'll fail.

All these prejudicial and discriminatory treatments create problems for everyone alike. People tend to believe that these problems exist only in others. That is not the case. Everyone has a part to play in promoting or perpetuating the problem. It will not be solved by inaction or ignoring it, hoping that it will go away. Awareness is the first step.

33

❋Story

Michael O'Brien, PhD.

When teen pop artist Britney Spears sang her hit, *"Oops, I Did It Again,"* she was articulating what executive coach Michael O'Brien tells executives—bad habits need to be broken. Lack of thoughtful management and uncontrolled emotions can spiral through a company, leading to employee mistakes, higher turnover, even reduced sales.

O'Brien has had several workplace incarnations, including ten years as a grocer-retailer, and years as a teacher, manager and university professor. He has a master's in education and a Ph.D. in corporate training and human resources development from the University of Cincinnati.

Question: You've said that for the average executive,

half of what he is doing is great stuff, 30 percent of his habits are not making any difference and 20 percent of his habits are holding people back. It seems that something you might be able to nibble at is the 30 percent that isn't making any difference.

Answer: Actually, what we usually start with are the habits that are holding people back, causing trouble. Our coaching is focused on helping people succeed within their business organizations, within the context of the business's goals. There are always revenue goals, but most sophisticated business people realize that you have to have a whole lot of other goals to get you to the revenue. It's a little risky to say: "Here are the five things that every business person can use."

· ·
BOOKS ON THE NIGHTSTAND

Working With Emotional Intelligence by Daniel Goleman

—*"Offers great insights into a domain many neglect."*

How The Irish Saved Civilization by Thomas Cahill

—*"I love history's transition periods; this shows how western*

civilization survived the Dark Ages."
· ·

We spend the bulk of our time with executives in large corporations so the store manager in a small town probably has a little bit of a different helping on his plate than the guy who runs an international company. We start by asking, "What are the business issues, what are the things getting in the way of success?" Then we look at what the executive is doing to contribute to those issues, his psychology, his way of thinking.

We use the metaphor of stories—"What is the story I'm telling myself that leads to behavior, which in turn brings results I do not want?" What are you telling yourself; what are you assuming to be true? We might observe a meeting, and we'll see where the executive is not communicating well with the people. He is missing their points. They are missing his points. They are on different planes. He is not reading the emotions in the room. One of the things we'll ask ourselves as coaches is, "What must this individual be thinking so that that behavior makes sense to him?" He is acting this way for some reason.

Q: You look, then, for the behavior behind a disconnect—the behavior behind why an executive missed something, missed a cue?

A: We look even behind that to the thinking behind a behavior or, said differently—what's 'the story'? The story has cognitive thoughts in it as well as emotions like fear and passion. There's something he has assumed to be true—call that 'the story'—out of which comes this behavior that is not working to produce the results he wants.

Part of what we do as coaches is we help people figure out that source. It's intuitive. It's unconscious. You don't even know it. When we start asking questions, we usually find out there is quite a complex story organized in there and when someone stands inside that story, the behavior makes a lot of sense. What the executive is not seeing is the effect his behavior is having on his people in the room, on the group, on the psychology, on what they're going to do next.

Q: You like to have clients keep a journal. Can you talk about how that helps identify their story?

A: We will pick an upset that occurred to them, something that just didn't work, and we'll say, "Go back and write out the story. What were you assuming to be true about those in the meeting room, about the purpose of the meeting? What were you assuming to be true about your role in all that?" If there is a big upset, we have them reflect on what the big upset reminds them of—in some cases, we have them go back and think about it as a child. What upsets you the most are things you learned to be upset about as a kid.

Q: The journal, then, should examine assumptions about what's true, assumptions about purpose of exchanges and assumptions of roles individuals have in the exchange. At that point, can an individual become reflective about their background?

A: When you do enough journaling, or sometimes in dialogue, what you begin to realize is that the executive has some responsibility in how things turned out. Usually when things don't go well, what's the first thing people do?

Q: I blame somebody else.

A: Exactly! You blame the other person or persons. Or people will rationalize, make up a story about how it wasn't really important or they didn't really care. The rationalization in the moment may make some sense, but it's coming out of an old fear or an unwillingness to address a difficult situation. All are perfectly normal human behaviors. Fears and reactions to fears are perfectly normal.

• •

BOOKMARKS

mgeneral.com
—*"Quick source for reviews, interviews and management e-books."*

travelocity.com
—*"Interesting meeting and vacation venues."*

hbr.org/forum
—*"Harvard Business Review discussions - fresh perspectives."*

• •

We try to help people get to a "discipline of personal mastery," and the first piece of that is self-awareness. "What are my thoughts, mental models and stories out of which comes my behavior, out of which comes some difference in the results occurring in the workplace?" For instance, the executive might realize that he set up the meeting in a way that affected his manager's behavior. The behavior brought poor results and eventually blame to that individual.

One of the tenets of the discipline of personal mastery is looking to see where an individual can be more accountable. A chief executive, a president, a vice president has to realize that their behavior has this huge symbolic effect on everybody else in the organization. A little, tiny thing—how you handle being upset in a meeting—will spread through the psychology of an organization like wildfire.

34

✲Desire

Tyrone Hill, *NBA Veteran and Entrepreneur*

Tyrone Hill did not grow up on a basketball court. In fact, this NBA rebounding great did not even begin to play basketball with any kind of serious intent until he was 16. After struggling with grades and working with tutors, he finally scored well enough on national aptitude tests to enroll at Xavier University.

After graduating, he played for a decade in the NBA before turning his back on the hardwood to fight through the hard knocks of business. In the highly competitive world of food vending, Hill's All-Star Vending brings healthy snacks and drinks to school vending programs.

But All-Star Vending brings more than snacks to schools.

The company has paid for school athletic uniforms and supplied nutrition bars before annual school-wide tests. And several times a year, Hill will make a personal appearance at his client schools to talk about why academic achievement is important.

Question: Let's see, 6,854 rebounds in your NBA career, 22,389 minutes of court time, that's pretty impressive right there. Are you going to miss the NBA?

Answer: And it's not just minutes, it's very high-level, focused minutes.

Am I going to miss it? I haven't missed it yet. Give me a chance to miss it. Give me a year to miss it. Most guys come out of retirement after their second year. Guys go back because they start missing it, you know.

CDs in the Changer

Lover's Rock and *Diamond Life* by Sade

Al Green's Greatest Hits by Al Green

Body Kiss by The Isley Brothers

Keep the Faith by Faith Evans

Q: Nutrition may be the great unwritten sports story of our time. When did you start paying attention to nutrition and diet and its impact on your ability to play?

A: I got into it early in my career. I got away from the pork, got away from the red meats. I might eat a steak once a month. I eat a burger every now and then, but I definitely don't have the pork in my diet at all. If I eat potatoes, it's mostly baked potatoes. I don't eat too many fried foods. I might eat some fried chicken. I might do that. When I'm at home in Atlanta, I'm into whole grain pancakes, the turkey sausage, egg whites, wheat toast. During lunch and dinner, I'm more into fish and chicken. Baked fish and a lot of salads. I eat a lot of pasta, too, but not too much of the creamy sauces.

Q: Tell me about the importance of nutrition for

children.

A: If you think about it, there are a lot of kids who have diseases like juvenile diabetes, who are over-weight and struggling with obesity. And there's not a lot of help for them. Lots of kids come from families that have some health issues. And they don't know much about nutrition. They're young, so you can't really blame them. There are a lot of factors. So, I figure if we can somehow start getting these kids eating right at an early age, if we get some discipline to it, the situation might improve.

But learning how to eat and what to eat, that is the challenge for companies like ours. We not only provide healthy drinks and snacks, but I come in and speak to the kids. They get to hear and see a public figure, who came from a public school system, talk about success, talk about applying themselves. I simply ask, "How bad do you want it?" I talk, too, about how important it is to eat right, how important it is to have proper hygiene, how important it is to be an all-around healthy person. When you're young you think you can do anything, eat anything. You know how it is with good, early habits. It sticks with you. It's hard to lose when you grow up in a family where you say, "Yes, Sir. Yes, Ma'am." These are habits that stick with you.

We offer to the schools a partnership with each individual school. With Withrow High School, we came in and gave the school several thousand energy bars in the fall and spring for their proficiency testing, and it helped raise test scores for that school. We'll do that at every school. We help pay for athletic uniforms—boys and girls. The golf outing raises funds for scholarship. We'll find other ways to generate monies for the school—silent auctions, for example.

Q: Why this business? A lot of pro athletes go into real estate. Why vending machines?

A: When I was little, I used to always run through the hallways at Withrow High School selling candy and sandwiches at lunch. For me and Felix (Felix Maye, president of All-Star Vending), it was a little entrepreneurship going on even then, back in ninth or tenth grade. I sold Snickers and Reese's Peanut

Butter Cups for a quarter each. Felix made the sandwiches at home. His mom would go buy the ham and cheese, the bread, and he would take orders. The next day, people would have their sandwiches. Kids did not want to eat the food from the cafeteria. We were probably making $50 to $60 a week. It cost $2.50 for a sandwich with a slice of tomato on it. One day we came up and started selling stuff and there was a domino effect.

BOOKS ON THE NIGHTSTAND

Life from Death Row by **Mumia Abu-Jamal**

Winning With Integrity: Getting What You Want Without Selling Your Soul by **Leigh Steinberg and Michael D'Orso**

Success Runs in Our Race: The Complete Guide to EffectiveNetworking in the Black Community by **George C. Frazer**

Now I have a landscaping company in Atlanta that is doing very well, but I wanted to go back to my roots, do something that could affect a lot of kids, a lot of people. Why not start a vending machine company that would not only benefit us but will benefit a lot of people? And it's something that's good for them—a vending machine company that doesn't sell a lot of chips and candy bars but goes to the opposite side of the spectrum with healthy snacks, milk, and sports drinks.

I come from a low-income family with a lot of health issues. You learn as you get older what's good for you. But when you're young, you don't care and have no idea. So if we can instill it now, hopefully we can help some of them.

Q: You were a great rebounder. Any similarities between rebounding and business?
A: Rebounding is about desire and determination. It's having a passion. When somebody has something they love to do, it becomes easier and easier. Another thing is this: every good shooter, every shot, he thinks he's going to make it. To

him, every shot is good before it leaves his hand. But every great rebounder sees it another way. To him, every shot is a missed shot. I don't think you can teach rebounding. It's something you have to love to do. You can teach somebody how to be in the right place or how to move their feet but rebounding has to be something that comes from within. You have to have heart.

I approach it the same way in the business world. You can't really be content. I made a great deal of money from basketball. I was blessed with playing professional basketball. Still, I want to make business money, too. And to do that, it's like rebounding. You've got to go get it. You have to envision the shots coming off the rim. In the heat of basketball game, I want seven or nine rebounds in the first half. Come the second half, I'm already at 14.

You have to have goals and you have to have a vision on the basketball court. It's the same in business.

Q: Five years from now, in the best of all possible worlds, what will your revenues be?

A: Oh, we'll be in the millions of dollars. In one year we went from two schools to 20. We now have contacts throughout the South and Midwest; Texas, Louisiana, North Dakota, Oklahoma, Maryland, Ohio, and schools we never thought we'd be in front of.

The scholarship program is critical because that offers young people a goal, and it's difficult to find and have goals in urban areas, where they are cutting programs all the time in schools in all of our cities. If a kid realizes that if they get straight A's and their attendance is good, then they get a $1,000 grant, well, that's attainable. It's an opportunity for people to look beyond, and we are going to mentor kids in the program. We are also talking to computer technology companies to partner with us to have technology centers brought up to where they need to be. If you don't have computer skills, you are going to be lost.

Q: Often in education, the difficulty for a teacher is simply finding and talking to the real contact person, the grandmother or somebody in the family, who expects and

sees to it that the homework gets done. Mom's doing a 2 to 11 at Wendy's.

A: Getting kids at the elementary level—that is the key. That's what All-Star vending is all about.

35

☀**High Octane**

Doug Newburg, Ph.D, *Director, Performance Education, University of Virginia School of Medicine.*

> *"Real competition is the competition between your vision and your skills - not between you and other people."*

> **—Doug Newburg**

Doug Newburg's research into athletics and professionals suggests that no matter the craft, high-octane performers have much in common. Most have a dream and are well-prepared to move toward it along a goal path. Obstacles only lead the committed to revisit those dreams.

Dr. Newburg, currently the director of Performance Education at the University of Virginia School of Medicine, believes top performers like musicians, surgeons, pilots, entertainers, and athletes, all share a trait of "resonance" —that is, a sustained energy flow linked to performance and engagement.

Question: What is resonance and how did the concept come about?

Answer: My favorite quote is from Hans-Georg Gadamer: "Relaxation is not the lack of effort but the absence of tension." That's the difference between high-level performers and the rest of us. High-level performers understand that. It's why Michael Jordan can make the last second shot. Most people who are good at hoops are good because it's the thing they love most in their life. That's how I was.

When I played basketball for the University of Virginia, I remember a game with Duke, my senior year. I was the guy who everyone cheered for to get in the game in the last minutes. We were up by 20 with about 10 minutes to go. I heard a woman sitting behind us say to her husband, "Let's start cheering to get Newburg in the game."

I looked at her and her husband looked at the scoreboard and said, "No, we don't have a big enough lead yet." So, finally, I got in and we won anyway. The next day in the *Washington Post,* the very first line was: "You knew victory was at hand when Virginia coach Terry Holland put in his human victory cigar, Doug Newburg."

Two years later I ran into the guy who wrote the article, John Feinstein, and he came running over to me and said he had just spent a year at Indiana University with the guys who sat at the end of the bench and that he didn't realize they had the same dream as the guys who actually played. I never thought about it like that—that I had the dream, too. But it got me thinking about why Virginia didn't win more championships.

Later, I was selling software and hated it so I went back to school to get a degree in sports psychology. I wanted to understand how to get people to perform better. It was my veterinarian who suggested I find five people who lived the way I wanted to live and look at what they did to get there, and if they were happy and fulfilled.

I started with Bruce Hornsby, the musician, Jeff Rouse, a gold medalist in the 1996 Olympics, and Kurt Tribble, a heart surgeon. These guys referred me to other people, and the next thing I knew, my life became about interviewing successful and happy people. What I found in talking to all these people was that performance is the creation and expression of ideas.

- -

CDs in the Changer

The Pretender by Jackson Browne

Live in San Diego by Sade

Dizzy Up the Girl by The Goo Goo Dolls

(What's the Story) Morning Glory by Oasis

Greatest Hits by Sly and The Family Stone

Break the Cycle by Stained

- -

The problem is that we start out doing things because we create our own ideas and, as we get better, we abandon those ideas for what we can get from the performance. Then we get serious and put pressure on ourselves. The essence of resonance is the thing you do in life to live the quote of Gadamer. Relaxation is not the lack of effort, but the absence of tension. All these performers told me that the more engaged they were, the more they enjoyed it and the better they performed.

Q: It seems to me that many high-powered and high-net worth people share this: they don't care about winning as much as they simply hate to lose.

A: I think it's both. If all you do is focus on how you hate to lose, you become fairly reactionary. We have a huge vocabulary for hating to lose, we call it obstacles and negativity, pressure and stress, but we don't have the same rich vocabulary for the positive side. It's not about winning. It's about playing to win.

Dawn Staley, head coach at Temple, was a two-time national player of the year in college hoops, and a point guard on the last two Olympic gold medal teams. She told me that winning the gold medal was the goal, but the reason she did what she did was her love for the competition. She said winning was nice, but that she did it for the experience of playing to win every day, the love of competing.

Q: When does desire become unhealthy? That is, when should a person realize that his dreams are not realistic, that his rock band won't be the Beatles?

A: I never looked at it that way. What they do and what I teach is, first of all—understand yourself. Most people can tell you what they don't want in life. But they can't tell you what they want in life because they don't know.

When I work with people, I tell them to pay attention and take notes about their daily routine, and to do it for two weeks straight. No judgments. Just take notes. Almost every day everybody has an experience that engages them, if only for a minute. They think it happens by accident. The bad stuff can be as momentary, yet it totally derails some people. If people spent the energy on going after what they want, that thing that engaged them, as opposed to the energy spent avoiding what they don't want, people would be a lot more successful.

Q: But these high-performers are resilient. Bruce Hornsby probably started off at a crummy little bar someplace, strumming a guitar with nobody listening, peanut shells on the floor.

A: And in a blue tuxedo. The reason I know Hornsby was that I played basketball in high school with his drummer, John Molo, who is now the drummer with Phil Lesh. Molo said it best. He said, "I know I get paid to ride the bus and be away from my family and get dehydrated." But he never confuses what he does for free with what he gets paid to do. He says he plays the drums for free. He gets paid for the other crap, the bus rides, being away from his family.

I was backstage watching him play with Bob Dylan about a year and a half ago. It was pretty amazing. What was so funny about it, I was sitting there on the side of the stage. It's about 100 degrees and 100 percent humidity and Dylan is dressed in full leather. And he's not sweating at all and Molo says, "Yeah, he's basically a wizard."

I've been backstage with Bonnie Raitt, the guys left over from the Grateful Dead, and the Allman Brothers. It's not what people think it is. Other than performing, the lifestyle can be fairly miserable. It's the same thing with athletes. I'd visit Ralph Sampson when he was playing for the Houston Rockets, and he's in a hotel room wide awake at 2 a.m. Or how about the surgeon who works 120 hours a week?

BOOKS ON THE NIGHTSTAND

The Autobiography of Quincy Jones

**The Witch Doctors: Making Sense of the Management Gurus
by John Micklethwait and Adrian Wooldridge**

It's Not About the Bike by Lance Armstrong;

Sting: Demolition Man by Christopher Sandford

It really speaks to your "hate-to-lose" thing, and I totally agree with you on that. The people who make it hate to lose. The people who don't make it are afraid of losing. Successful people understand bad things can happen, but they also understand that it's not going to prevent them from doing what they want to do. They don't worry about that stuff. They prepare to feel the sense of profound esthetic happiness and they perform better.

Q: Can sports function as a development tool?

A: Anything can, really. Do you enjoy the act of improving your skills toward your vision? What I would argue is that the vision most people have about success is just wrong. Think about goals we go after: good grades, good college, good job, good car, get married, get a mortgage and have kids. A lot of people have done those things and have no idea what is next, other than to get more money. Success is not a destination; it's an experience. I hate when people say it's a journey. It's an experience. It's not a thing to achieve, yet that is how so many people view it.

The people I've interviewed are the best in the world at

what they do. Yet, they've never thought in any serious way about winning a gold medal, winning a Grammy award, or becoming chief executive officer. What happened was they loved doing something in the early stages of their career. It fascinated them. The more they did it, the better they got and the more energy they gained from doing it.

Q: Do athletes make better employees because they inherently understand concepts of discipline, delayed gratification, teamwork and competition?

A: No, not at all. It's not true. People want to believe that sports are good for you. I've been around enough really successful athletes and coaches. I did a workshop for the Olympic coaches before the 2000 Olympics, and what I hear all the time is that organized anything has the potential to become about the system prospering at the expense of the individual. I don't see any more value being an athlete on a team than being a musician or being a student. Being true to your calling, that's what's important.

My full-time job is to look for new resident docs at the hospital. We don't look for the skills people bring, tests and grades; we look for people who have a low buzz of energy. No matter what happens to that person, they do not lose sight of how important that low buzz of energy is. They don't have *low* lows the way most people have. They're steady. They're focused. The phrase that sums it up: *It's easier to take someone who is and teach them to know than to take someone who knows and teach them to be.*

· ·

ON THE COFFEE TABLE

Esquire and *ESPN Magazine*

· ·

In most corporations I've worked with, most executives and middle managers won't make time, or promote, or reward people, for playing to win. Rather, they impose what they themselves have been taught all their life on the people below them. They want different results, but they don't let anybody do anything different to achieve those results.

When I sold software, my manager said I was to make 30 calls a day and do this and do that. I started watching the guys who never worried about quotas but always met their quota. Well, they weren't doing any of that stuff. They worked half as hard as I did. What they did was love the relationship they had with their customers. They'd call and talk to them and go see them. The more they did that, when it came down to buying a software product, the customer bought from the guy they liked. No one ever told me that.

I've done work for the FBI, I've worked in medicine and in business, education and sport. I've been on an aircraft carrier talking to pilots. What I've found is that the people who are the best, they figure out what's really important and focus on that. The rest of us are so worried about something going wrong, trying to prevent bad things from happening that we are taking our energy away from making the right things happen.

36

✳The Brand

Donald J. Trump

For real estate mogul Donald Trump, money is just one way to keep score. One of the nation's first real estate developers to recognize the power of brand, Trump decided early on in his career that he would turn his personality, his name and his presence into a brand. The rest would follow.

With estimates of his net worth ranging from $2 billion to $6 billion—and debt in the same range—Trump has an A-list of tenants in his New York City properties, a jet-setting roster of golfers who are members of his country club projects and, when he goes golfing, he tees it up with an A-list of celebrities too, from Greg Norman to Annika Sorenstam and Nick Faldo.

A telephone conversation with him can be like trying to

juggle jungle bats or attempting to stuff six mice into a bag with one hand. Lots of activity but not a lot of results. And he gives the phrase "New York Minute" new meaning. Some interviews last a New Jersey nanosecond:

Question: Our paths have crossed before in Miami during the Bengals/49ers Super Bowl, back in 89-90, I believe. I was interviewing somebody while seated in the aisle next to you and the police didn't like it, then we chatted about the project you had in Cincinnati.

Answer: Yes, I remember. I remember. A lot of time has passed since then.

Q: Yes it has. So, can we first talk about risk? How do you measure risk associated with a project?

A: Well, there are risks associated with almost anything you do. A man who lives in Cincinnati who I have a great deal of respect for is Carl Lindner. I don't know if you know Mr. Lindner but he's a great guy and somebody who knows a great deal about business. He's an amazing man.

· ·

CDs in the Changer

The Essential Tony Bennett

Sinatra Reprise: The Very Good Years

Tumbleweed Connection **by Elton John**

Cieli di Toscana **by Andrea Bocelli**

Romantica: The Very Best of Luciano Pavarotti

· ·

Q: I believe Mr. Lindner has segued away from big real estate projects.

A: Well, it's a specialty, a real specialty, no question about it. Carl is a real good friend of mine and he's gotten into a lot of unbelievable things. I think real estate was never his big thing —although he's made money in real estate. He's made money in a lot of things he's done.

Q: Obviously you've made a little bit of money in real estate. What are the elements you look for in a project? Ten years down the road? Ten months down the road?

A: Well, I think it depends on where and it depends on what. We have a lot of projects going right now. A big one in Chicago. A big one in California, along the ocean. A lot of them are going on in New York. I'm building one in Miami. They're all good. And again, if the markets change, they probably won't be so good. But right now, the markets where we are at—they are very strong.

· ·

BOOKS ON NIGHTSTAND

Winning: The Ultimate Business How-to Book
by Jack Welch and Suzy Welch

My Life by Bill Clinton

My American Journey: An Autobiography by Colin Powell

· ·

Q: I didn't hear Cincinnati. I didn't hear Des Moines. I didn't hear about any mid-sized Midwestern markets there in that list.

A: Well, I would do one in Cincinnati. I think Cincinnati is a great place. It's the Queen City. It's been a favorite of mine. I lived there, literally, for about a year. Boy, it was probably in the early 70's. It was a great place.

Is the Maisonette still there? Still a great restaurant? They had great food. Great dining. If the right opportunity presented itself in a Midwestern city, I would certainly look at it.

Q: If you look out across the history of American real estate development, the project that has never failed to bring in high-net-worth individuals is a golf course: hotels, housing, other investments. Will mid-sized cities begin to encourage golf course construction right downtown?

A: Well, I think they're going to start to, at least more so than in the past because of certain things that have taken place. But the golf industry, generally speaking, is not very robust. It's a relatively small industry. You do a course, it's not a big project, and it's not that easy to pull off, environmentally or in other ways.

Q: You have thousands of people working for you. When you hire, are you looking for credentials? Or are you looking for commitment? Are you looking for education? Can you look into a person's eyes to see their heart?

A: I think I see a lot. There's nothing like education. It's a great thing. But it's not exclusively that. If someone went to the Wharton School of Finance or Harvard, certainly it tells you that they've done a good job and that they're smart, but it's not exclusively that.

. . . .

FAVORITE MEAL

Meatloaf, mashed potatoes and a dessert of cherry-vanilla ice cream.

. . . .

Q: When you hire staff, do you look for people with families, single people, or does it matter?

A: Oh, I think the family is always a good thing. It's always an asset. There's nothing bad about it. Are you talking about it from the standpoint of a person having family or from the standpoint of hiring somebody with family?

It's always nice to hire somebody with family. It means they're supporting more than themselves, and they'll be a little more cautious.

Q: Will we see you in Cincinnati anytime soon?

A: It very could well be. Maybe I'll go to a Reds game with Carl Lindner. I have great respect for Mr. Lindner, and I have great respect for the job he's done.

Q: If you're in town, call. I know some guys. I'm pretty sure I can get us a tee time at the Camargo Club.

A: Well that sounds good. That sounds very good. You take care of yourself, okay?

37

❋Let Go

Hale Dwoskin

Letting go of grudges, animosity, jealousy or resentment is a tough act for people. Hale Dwoskin is the president and chief executive of *The Sedona Method* and a popular consultant who works with individuals and companies on how to release stress, ill-will, and other impediments to success. His *Sedona Method: Your Key to Lasting Happiness, Success, Peace and Emotional Well-Being* offers a solution for executives and their pressure-cooker lives that involves "letting go."

Employees operate under the same equation as their bosses. Stress is at an all-time high. Many workers fear that a pink slip is days, weeks or a few months away, and the pressure to do more with less has rippled across factory floors and through office cubicles alike. Dwoskin offers a way out.

• •

CDs in the Changer

World Chants by **Krishna Das**

A Day Without Rain: The Best of Enya

Music Detected by **Deep Forest**

• •

Question: Are we all that stressed out? What does your Sedona Method have to offer?

Answer: The Sedona Method has been around for 30 years but this is the first time it's been in a book. [It] is the ultimate cure for desk rage, interoffice politics and work-related stress. This approach has a positive reputation with millions of people all over the country, and the reason it's so popular is that it's both very timely and very effective. People are in pain, and the Sedona Method is a very, very simple, yet powerful way to let go of that emotional pain.

What's unique about it is that it doesn't require you to relive past experience or figure out why you're suffering. It just shows you how to let it go. If you think about it, our country has tremendous financial abundance, yet at the same time, we're suffering from stress and anxiety and depression and extreme anger.

We did a study recently and found that 45 percent of households in America have at least one person who has a severe anger problem. We also found that 36 percent of the people in the U.S. have a problem with stress. Our society has stress built into it. The approach also appeals equally to men and women and does not require journaling. It does not require sharing with others what's bothering you. It helps you to master your emotions without going through the drama.

Q: What is the genesis of the Sedona Method?

A: In 1952, at the age of 52, Lester Levenson was sent home to die from his second coronary. The doctor gave him weeks to live, but he didn't give up. He went back to the web within himself and discovered that we all have a natural ability to let go of unwanted emotions. He used this approach intensely on himself, and in just three months, he went from a physical and emotional basket-case to perfect health [during which] he found a profound state of happiness. Levenson lived another 42 years. The techniques he developed and used on himself form the basis of the Sedona Method.

There are several things people can do.

First of all, we treat feelings as though we are the feeling. Also, we treat these feelings as facts. Feelings are just feelings. They're not you. They're not facts. And you can easily let them go. And there are simple things you can do to let go of feelings.

The first step is to acknowledge what you're already feeling. Step Two is to understand why you feel that way. Step Three is simply to ask, *Could I let this feeling go?* Step Four is asking yourself, *Would I let it go?* Step Five is to ask, *When?*

Most of us make up stories about why we feel how we feel, and it's just an excuse to hold on to our pain and our suffering. But you have to let go of needing to understand the reasons, the source of the pain and suffering. We might never get there. Our process makes it easy to decide to just let it go.

· ·

Books on the Nightstand

Harry Potter and the Order of the Phoenix by J.K. Rowling

The Da Vinci Code by Dan Brown

The 72 Names of God: Technology for the Soul
by Yehunda Berg and Rav Berg

I Am That: Talks With Sri Nisargadatta
by Nisargadatta Maharaj

· ·

All of this has changed lives and, if we had a few days, I could tell you story after story after story about how it's turned lives around. Part of the reason we hold onto our feelings is we think we're justified. We'd rather be right than free of our pain. It's human nature.

Q: So we're all a bunch of petulant 2-year-olds?

A: People come into this world with great openness, but around 2, 2 1/2, we start to protect everything as though it belongs to us. We start to think that we're the center of the universe. Obviously we're not. What happens when you let go of the emotions that are pulling you back to the past, when you let go of the emotions of wanting to change what's already happened, and the desire to control what's yet to come, is that you find yourself relaxed, open and at ease in the current moment.

Mutual of New York did a study of field underwriters— euphemism for sales people. They took a group, taught them the Sedona Method, and that group outperformed a group that had no training, by 33 percent over a six-month period. That's not the only thing unique. The study was broken down into two three-month segments. The increase after three months was 23 percent, but it was somewhere in the 43 percent range for the second period. It was increasing over time. That is very rare.

Q: Why has the Sedona Method resonated?

A: It's simple. Most self-improvement efforts have a lot of things that cause them to fail. One is complexity; they are impossible to do without help. The Sedona Method is so easy, it's almost impossible to forget once you learn it. The second thing that causes self-improvement methods to fail is the belief that you're broken and need to be fixed. Then you're always broken, so no matter what you do, it's not going to be good enough. The Sedona Method is based on the premise that you are already whole, complete and perfect. You simply need to uncover that.

In addition to being complex, most self-improvement techniques are difficult. Once you learn the Sedona Method, it becomes as easy and as second nature as breathing. And today, these simple principals that we have talked about have come right out of the book and they are enough to make an enormous difference in people's lives.

38

✴Invent

Robert Robinson Sr., *KaiVac*

Figuring out a better way to clean toilets led Ohio inventor Robert Robinson Sr. to create a system that turned around the fortunes of his family-owned janitorial supply company, brought thousands of American companies cleaner buildings and gave their workers spotless restrooms.

KaiVac Inc. is the perfect example of a company finding a niche and revenues in a commonplace process that had been overlooked for eons: a better way to clean toilets. At the heart of the KaiVac system is an innovative, all-in-one machine. More than 10,000 units have been sold since its first incarnation in 1997.

Today, KaiVac posts revenues of $7 million and offers

America's custodians a hands-free process to clean bathrooms, hallways and walls and in so doing, brings some long-lost dignity back into their job description. Robinson sees a national and international market of more than $200 million for their ground-breaking commercial and institutional process.

Question: So how did you go from a mid-level engineer at a struggling paper mill to an inventor of an innovative machine that cleans restrooms and buildings?

Answer: I was a mechanical engineer and was not very happy. Day after day I'd come home, and my wife would tell me that they could really use an engineer at her family's janitorial supply company. She'd say she started off [the day] answering the phone, but by the end of the day she was delivering toilet paper to companies. That's what they did. I'd think, *Well, what kind of way is that to make a living?*

But I was 28 years old, and I thought that I'd give this supplies and sales thing a whirl. I came here, and I'd go to these conventions of other engineers and hear people saying, "What do you do for a living?"

One guy would be with IBM, another guy would say he was with another Fortune 500 company, and they'd turn to me and say, "What do you do, Bob?"

"Oh, I'm in chemicals," I'd say. I was so embarrassed that I was selling toilet paper, buckets, mops and bowl cleaners. Anyhow, the business started growing. I stuck with it and got into systems, because there is a system for how to clean a bathroom, how to clean the bowls, how to clean the floors.

In the early 1990's, I started a side business cleaning grocery stores. My father-in-law, Walter Green, was retired. He started his company in desperation when he lost his job in the 1960s. He bought a couple cases of toilet paper and some cleaners and started selling out of his garage; now that's guts and courage.

Cleaning grocery stores was kind of sexy for the engineer in me. We had power equipment and automatic scrubbers, propane burnishers, walk-behind equipment, and my engineering background started to come out. It was better than selling mops and buckets and paper towels.

That's when I learned that chemicals and equipment don't clean buildings, people do. It's all about having the right people, having the right training program and really, that's when I got my education, putting all these products and people together into a systematic approach.

So during the day, we're selling janitorial supplies. At night, I'm working the third shift cleaning supermarkets. It was literally running me ragged. That's when I really began to understand the plight of the worker. A typical, commercial cleaning worker will clean 25,000 to 30,000 square feet on a typical shift—that's about ten average houses. And no matter how you cut it, it's hard work. And then you have to deal with store managers.

- -

CDs in the Changer

Soundtracks from *Gladiator* and *Braveheart*

Vineyard Church Praise Songs

A Day Without Rain **by Enya**

Contemporary Christian Music

- -

Picture it. There's a guy who cleans all night long. He has a machine break down so he's got to mop the floor by hand, and then this manager shows up in the morning and he cusses you out and calls you a stinking, f-ing janitor. I was never treated more like a dog in all my life and yet I had to work so hard. Janitors are seen as low-lifes. They are the lowest rung on the socio-economic ladder. I'm seeing this and I'm getting a heart for the worker about this time.

Well, we got fired because we weren't that great. I was like, "Thank God." But that's where I learned chemicals, equipment and how people clean. It was a whole process. That's where I learned it all. So we took the approach to schools, rather than grocery stores, and we found that schools were desperately in need of training.

Most schools have in-house cleaning, but their approach is 30 years in the past. And I started reading the literature and found that the number one complaint in our industry from clients was not floors, it was bathrooms: dirty, stinking, rotten, filthy bathrooms or—as they always phrased it—"A lack of restroom cleanliness."

Once I called the editor of a trade journal and asked for the previous 10 years of surveys and sure enough, the number one problem was bathrooms. I turned to my sales guys and said, "Fellows, we've got to start focusing on bathrooms. The bigger the problem, the bigger the opportunity."

What I found was there is never a clean bathroom in the commercial world. The training is always, *here's the bowl cleaner, here's the disinfectant, go figure it out*. That is not a job to inspire people to greatness. I mean, I was even embarrassed selling toilet paper. But we purposely said, "Let's figure this out—and figure it out before our competition."

Q: When did the revelation hit you that something needed to be done? What was your pivot point?
A: I'll never forget this one day. I'm showing these three or four janitors how to clean a toilet. I'm in a filthy bathroom with a quart of bowl cleaner. I don't know if you've ever read the instructions on how to clean a toilet but you take your Johnny Mop and push the level of the water down. You push three times. So I'm on my hands and knees and my knees are in urine and some toilet water splashes on my face and I get this overwhelming sense of shame: I hate this. My nose is where somebody's butt just was, and I realized there has to be a better way to do this.

I really felt for these three guys who were standing there watching. Here I am, some guy who's all dressed up showing these three dejected guys how to clean a filthy bathroom. There's urine on the walls. There's disease, mold and mildew.

I got up and walked out of there and told myself that I was going to figure out a better way to do this. I went to a local school district and asked them if I could clean their bathrooms for the next 30 days. They were like, "Please, clean the whole district for the next 30 days."

I told my sales guys to meet me and that we were going to clean their bathrooms, but we were not going to take a mop, bowl cleaner or Johnny Mop with us because mops never worked; you swish around dirty water, you can't get into corners. Then you drag it down the hallway and into the kitchen and classrooms? These are ancient tools.

So we went in there with pressure washers, wet vacuums, rubber squeegees, sprayers, and a stop watch.

We found out some interesting stuff: a 3,000 pound per square inch pressure washer, man, it really does clean. But it also peels the tiles off the floor, knocks ceramic loose from the walls, and it can really make a mess of a bathroom. It was too much pressure. We found that wet vacuums work, but you can never find all the pieces to go with the hoses because they're scattered throughout the buildings.

And this is where the light bulb came on. What if we combined a small pressure washer with a wet vacuum, and plenty of hose all on one platform placed at the doorway?

So you come in and spray cleaning, disinfectant chemicals on the sinks, toilets, walls and floors. Turn the chemicals off and splash on the water. Of course the drains won't work because they're always higher than the rest of the floor, so you have a wet-vac squeegee right on the unit to suck it all up. And after 30 days of messing around, we came up with a system that solved all the issues. We got a patent and I found I do have an aptitude for thinking out-of-the box.

I'll never forget the date: it came to us on April 27, 1997.

Q: What was it that came alive? The mechanical engineer in you or could anybody have come up with this system, if they'd only taken the time to do what you did?

A: What happened was we were intensely focused on the problem. Funny how I didn't start inventing things until I was in my 40s, but I never thought of putting a patent on anything. Many systems we've developed are now patent protected. I do have that aptitude for invention. We have five patents now and six or seven patents pending. We innovate here.

Q: What is it with KaiVac? What's the name mean?

A: Keep At It. Keep Always Improving, Keep Attempting the Impossible. Kick Ass Invention. I found this Greek word

Kairose: it's when a great thing happens at just the right time and just the right place; the fall of the Soviet Union, the invention of penicillin.

Then I'm at a show, and a little Hawaiian lady comes up to me and asks if I knew that Kai meant the great blue ocean. But we got our name because Kai as a company name was already taken so we came up with KaiVac. There are so many weird things that came together to make this happen.

Let me give you some numbers. Just in our area we have 70 schools districts that have a KaiVac. There are 120,000 school buildings in the United States. For every million people, there are 420 school buildings. One of our goals is to have multiple KaiVacs in each school building because this does more than just clean bathrooms. We focused on bathrooms and schools because they are heavy-duty. This could go in a lot of different directions. But we've found great resistance in the industry to the KaiVac. It's disruptive innovation. It obsoletes equipment and requires new thinking and investment.

BOOKS ON THE NIGHTSTAND

The Bible

Leadership books by Tom Peters, John Maxwell, Jim Collins

Leading the Revolution **by Gary Hamel**

Christian Themed Books by John Eldridge

Naked Economics: Undressing the Dismal Science
by Charles Wheelan

So our challenge became selling this to an industry that is extremely slow to change. We are change freaks and have changed the KaiVac three or four hundred times. I can't sleep at night unless I'm tweaking something. With a big company changes happen slowly. But here, being a small company, we can change quickly.

Ultimately, KaiVac is doing for the janitor what the bulldozer did for the ditch-digger. This is an industry that hasn't changed for centuries. I mean, the greatest innovation in this industry was a rag on the end of a stick—a mop. That was innovation. Clean the castle and swab the deck. It's the way it's always been. But KaiVac is going to change that, one building at a time.

A janitor is a guy with a ball cap on backwards; he's wearing dirty blue jeans, dragging a dirty mop bucket with a big key ring on his hip. How many kids want to grow up to be a janitor? Not very many. But we're changing that.

Every time I fly into a city I look down as we're about to land and see big buildings, parking lots and people. Anywhere you have that combination you can point and go KaiVac, KaiVac, KaiVac. Every mall? KaiVac. Every fast food restaurant? KaiVac. Anywhere floors are swept or cleaned with a mop in filthy water—KaiVac. This is going to change how we clean, and it's going to raise the custodian into an environmental technician. It's going to inspire pride. This is a way to clean bathrooms without touching them and in one-third of the time, while raising the dignity of your workers.

Schools hear that, they go, "Wow," because the increase in productivity allows one person to do more, to finally get to the lightbulbs that need to be changed, to the walls that need to be painted. We are bringing meaning to the phrase, "The last shall be first."

39

❋Big Steel Blues

Daniel R. DiMicco, *Nucor*

"The American dream is something we live, not something we buy. Manufacturing is critical to preserving that dream."

—Daniel R. DiMicco

Nucor Inc. emerged from the 1990s as the giant of American steel companies and a symbol of how a company can blow past good to become great. The Charlotte, North Carolina-based Nucor is led by Daniel R. DiMicco, a vice chairman and chief executive who started out at the company in 1982 as a plant metallurgist and chief of quality control at a Nucor Steel plant in Plymouth, Utah.

A Brown University and University of Pennsylvania graduate with Bachelor and Master degrees in engineering, metallurgy and materials science, DiMicco bases employee relations at non-union Nucor on four principles: managers must manage so employees have the opportunity to earn according to their productivity; work done well today leads to a guarantee of a job tomorrow; employees have the right to be treated fairly and must believe that they will be treated fairly; there must be an avenue of appeal for workers who feel they have been wronged.

While more than 40 steel companies went bankrupt in the U.S. in recent years, Nucor has found profits in every quarter since 1956. It has offered cash dividends every quarter for 125 consecutive quarters. Today, no longer a metallurgist in a grimy steel plant, DiMicco is a straight-talking executive who punctuates his words with *deeez* and *doze*, not *these* and *those*.

Question: How has manufacturing swooned and why? Why is it such a vital industry for the American economy?

Answer: Make no mistake about it, while manufacturing may be 14 percent of gross domestic product, it is 20 percent of the jobs in this country and that 20 percent is among the higher paying jobs in the United States. And if you take a look at indirectly—all of the businesses that thrive off manufacturing—you'll see it's a sector that has an impact on 40 percent of our GDP. Right now, the deck is stacked against the future success of manufacturing in this country.

The first thing I always do when I talk about this is I take my clothes off—to a point. **[He begins to shed his sports coat, takes off his tie and rolls up his sleeves.]** This is the steel business. It's a tough business. It's a cleaner business than it used to be, but it's still a dirty, hot business. At Nucor we don't wear jackets and we don't wear ties. And in this business, you damn well better roll up your sleeves and get down to it, whether you're the CEO or the newest employee hired into one of our operations anywhere in the country.

The problems that U.S. manufacturers face are serious, perhaps as serious as they've ever been, but they are by no means hopeless. The difficulties result not from failures of American companies or American workers—although there have been some—but rather from the policies of a global trading system. The deck is stacked against U.S. manufacturers.

Q: Why can't privately owned steel companies compete on the world stage?

A: In the steel business, we've been playing against a stacked deck for a long time, but particularly since 1996. For decades, steel mills around the world have been built and sustained with government money. You have to understand that throughout most of the world, and I mean most of the world, manufacturing companies, whether it be steel or otherwise, are government-owned entities. They are not free-market business enterprises.

In China, 80 percent of the manufacturing is owned by the Chinese government. They get all kinds of tax forgiveness, subsidies. They manipulate the currency. So right from the get-go, they have a 50 percent cost advantage over the guy in the United States who is making the same widget. Forget about labor cost issues, regulatory issues, energy, healthcare costs. Forget about all that. They have a 50 percent cost advantage because they manipulate their currency.

Part of their strategy is to create a manufacturing base, create lots of employment. And there's nothing wrong with that, but there's a right way to do it and a wrong way to do it. There's a legal way to do it and an illegal way to do it. People need to play by the same rules. If you don't, you have independent businesses fighting for capital in markets where the capital is provided free to others. Loans are never expected to be repaid.

It hasn't changed to this day in places like China and India. It's not a question of U.S. manufacturers competing on a level playing field with other manufacturers. We are fighting other governments day in and day out, no mistake about it.

When demand crashed in Asia as a result of a currency crisis, steel from all over the world flooded the U.S., much of it dumped at subsidized prices. This torrent of imports simply overwhelmed American steel-makers. Let me be blunt. By the end of 2001, much of our steel capacity was very close to shutting down for good, an outcome that would have crippled one of our nation's foundational industries and threatened our national security and economic leadership. If there was ever an industry that needed a type of temporary tariff relief, implemented by President Bush in March of 2002, it was the steel industry.

The fact is that all manufacturers are hurting, but what pains me the most about steel critics is that they are playing into the hands of those in Washington who don't want to do anything for American manufacturers.

When we fight amongst ourselves, we send the message that it's easier to do nothing, that looking for policy answers is more trouble than it's worth at a time when U.S. manufacturers are looking for the government to come up with creative solutions and policy initiatives. It's the worst possible message to send.

Q: But Nucor has never been a company that runs to the government for help.

A: Things have gotten so bad and so unbalanced that even companies like Nucor have to stand up and say, "We're mad as hell and we're not going to take it anymore."

It's not just Nucor. It's not just the steel industry. It's manufacturers of all sizes, shapes and types of products who are standing up to say [that]. Benjamin Franklin said, "We must all hang together or most assuredly we will all hang separately." We must learn from farmers. I'm not talking about subsidies. Agriculture accounts for one-tenth as much as our GDP as manufacturing. But by standing together, the farmers have much more clout in Washington than we do. Much more.

Q: What should the message be?

A: First, we have to let Washington know that the manufacturing crisis is real, despite a couple of months where we've seen some improvement. It's not cyclical. It's not imagined. It's not going away on its own. Beginning July 2000 through July 2004, the manufacturing sector lost jobs for 45 months in a row. That's 45 months in a row. It totals 2.9 million manufacturing jobs, more than one-seventh of all manufacturing jobs in this country. It's an enormous figure. Over the last three-and-a-half years, 10 percent of U.S. manufacturing capacity has been idled.

Almost two-and-a-half years after the end of the current U.S. recession, we are still seeing only mild growth in manufacturing output. This has been the weakest manufacturing recovery since 1919! History is repeating itself.

U.S. manufacturers cannot even take advantage of the improving global economy. Last year world merchandise trade increased by four percent, but U.S. manufacturing exports actually declined for the third year in a row. There is no question that our trade balance is a major part of the crisis. Our trade deficit for the month is the highest it's ever been: just shy of $49 billion. In the 1990s, we had trade deficits that were in the hundreds of millions of dollars, and that was for the year. Now it's $49 billion for one month? Phew, it sends chills down my spine.

Q: With imports crippling so many sectors and with trade deficits setting new records every year and every month, talk about the jobs lost to foreign competition. Measuring the loss is complicated.

A: One study estimated that between 1994 and 2000, imports eliminated approximately 5.8 million jobs. It's a fact. Even after accounting for jobs created for exports, this study concluded that the growing trade deficit eliminated, net total, 3 million actual potential jobs from the U.S. economy, most of them high-paying manufacturing jobs. In the U.S economy, 150,000 jobs have to be created each and every month just to create zero progress, just to stay in place, just to hold our own because our population is growing.

There are some fundamental issues that are going to sink long-term recovery and sink our manufacturing sector. The problem is, when it's gone, it will be too late to bring it back.

Q: Some might claim that there is no crisis, that manufacturing no longer matters and the competitive advantage lies elsewhere.

A: Anybody who lives in a community or has a job involved in manufacturing would not understand that argument. So much of our history of who we are, what this great nation is, centers around what we make and what we create. There has to be a reason why the rest of the world wants to duplicate what we've done here and are willing to do it to the extent that it will destroy what we have here.

What are we missing? Why are we so willing to give up what everybody else in the world wants? There is something wrong—big time.

Industries and livelihoods change, for sure. But to change from a nation that makes things to one that does not, to become a country that simply manages, services, sells or repackages what others produce? It's a change that I don't want to be around to see.

We've all been told that out-sourcing our manufacturing base means low-cost goods for Americans. But the United States is not just a collection of 280 million consumers. Cheapest possible T-shirt? Cheapest possible television set? Cheapest vegetables? No, this is our home. It's where we raise our children, help our neighbors, build our churches, and bury our dead. It's a great nation and civilization.

Americans have worked and struggled for over 200 years to create a healthy and balanced society. Not just for a few wealthy Americans, but for all Americans. The American dream is something we live, not something we buy. Manufacturing is critical to preserving that dream. It has consistently provided high-paying jobs and served as the backbone for our country. Manufacturing has supported the middle class in this country and offered a promise to families to improve their standard of living, send their children to school, and provide for a reasonable retirement.

We literally cannot defend ourselves without manufacturing. We are the only world superpower at an exceedingly dangerous point in world history—and you can argue about the politics of what's going on—that cannot make enough ammunition to supply what is not a full-out war. You can't order these things from other countries unless we want to give those other countries a veto over our foreign policy. To remain truly independent, we have to be able to make these things ourselves and that alone requires a strong manufacturing base. We need balance.

Q: What happens to those Americans left behind when manufacturing moves off-shore?

A: We've seen what happens when thousands of manufacturing jobs are lost. We've seen the increase in crime. We've seen the empty homes left behind that once sheltered productive citizens who had to leave to seek new work. We've seen the pain and the humiliation of proud men and women who cannot support their families. We know that America can not simply bid good riddance to its manufacturing base, to the millions of jobs supported by manufacturing, as well as the towns and communities that depend on those jobs. There are enormous social consequences.

It galls me when I hear some politicians say what we really need to do is set up these re-training programs for all those folks losing their jobs. Damn them. The hell with that. What we really need is to create the jobs, to hold onto the jobs that are disappearing because of unfair and illegal trading practices. To simply say re-training is the solution to the problem? It makes me sick to my stomach.

Q: How do you replace the jobs once they are gone?

A: Well, it's comforting to think that we will all become entrepreneurs or inventors for the rest of the world. Or get service sector jobs catering to those who do. Who are we kidding? While we are congratulating each other on how creative and intelligent we are, how many of those jobs and skills associated with the information age are headed in the same direction as manufacturing activity?

A recent study from a high-tech consulting firm predicts that in the next 15 years, American employers will move about 3.3 million white-collar service jobs and $136 billion in wages abroad. Another study reports that financial service companies alone plan to move more than 500,000 jobs off-shore in the next five years.

I see it every day in Charlotte, North Carolina—the second largest banking center in the United States of America—as they out-source their information technology and other services to India and around the world. The Information

Technology Association of America reports that 22 percent of large technology companies are already moving jobs offshore.

Take a look at where a lot of that technical engineering and drafting work is being done today. It's headed to India and Asia and places where they are smart and eager and willing to absolutely monopolize those areas if they can. Assuming that service workers and professionals are insulated from the same economic factors that are hurting manufacturing would be a catastrophic mistake.

Let me put it to you a little differently. Scotty, in *Star Trek*, has a pretty fancy piece of equipment. It is a Beam-Me-Up-Scotty machine. He could move solid objects just about anywhere.

Do you know how difficult, complicated, and expensive it is to ship solid products around the world? Do you know how difficult it is to ship 24-ton coil from China to the United States? The energy consumed, the ocean-going vessels needed, the pollution generated when it's produced in China instead of the United States where the regulations are more stringent?

Do you have any idea how difficult it is to move product from A to B, to load it, unload it, put it on another truck, then a railcar, then ship it, and the damage it might sustain? It's not an easy thing to do, but we do it every day and we've gotten damn good at it. But it's not an easy thing to do. We've done it. And we've done it without the Beam-Me-Up-Scotty machine. But can you imagine how much faster and more efficient all that transportation of solid goods would be if we had a Beam-Me-Up-Scotty machine?

Well, we have a Beam-Me-Up-Scotty machine that folks use everyday for information, knowledge, and money flows. It's called a computer. A CEO of a corporation doesn't have to be in Charlotte. Neither does the CEO of the Bank of America or Wachovia. They don't have to be here. The electronic transfer of information happens like the Beam-Me-Up-Scotty machine— high-quality, low-cost transfers.

If you don't think those jobs servicing information are going to disappear ten times as fast, 1,000 times as fast as manufacturing jobs— where we have to deal with moving huge objects around the world—you're kidding yourself and so are our politicians and the leaders of this country. They're kidding themselves—whether they are Democrat or Republican—they're kidding themselves.

Q: Some claim that the current crisis hits only the so-called traditional industries and the U.S manufacturers need to be more high-tech.

A: The premise of that argument is all wrong. You can no longer draw an easy distinction between old-fashioned, traditional manufacturing and modern, high-tech manufacturing. Compare the car you drive today to the car you drove 10 years ago. Today's cars ride better, handle better, last longer, have better sound systems. They can even tell you when you make a wrong turn. And, of course, it's made from a lot better steel. All of these improvements resulted from research and development using the latest technology.

- -
CDs in the Changer

Best of the 50s, 60s, 70s by Various Vrtists

Muddy Waters, The Anthology 1947-1972
- -

Two thirds of U.S. research and development spending and 90 percent of new patent approvals take place in manufacturing. What are we going to lose if we don't un-stack the deck? In the modern world, all manufacturing has to be high-tech. Whether you're making steel or forging, or making an automobile, it's all high-tech.

You ought to see how steel is made today at one of our plants. You might as well be in a Ford or General Motors assembly plant. If you define a certain class of industry as high-tech, you'll find that they are in trouble, too. U.S. trade in advanced technology went from a $19 billion surplus in 1999 to a $16 billion deficit last year. Since January 2001, the United States has lost 228,000 semi-conductor and electronic component manufacturing jobs, 76,000 computer equipment-making positions and over 86,000 communications equipment jobs. High-tech companies are facing the same crisis as the rest of us.

Sure, you can point to some industries in trouble, but the politicians will say, "Here are five examples of manufacturers that did well last year." You can always find a few bright spots in the midst of any disaster. Even the Detroit Tigers won 43 games last year. If you only looked at those games, you might conclude that they had a pretty good year, but, unfortunately for the Tigers, you can't base your assessment on just those games. And you can't base your policies on those few companies that are bucking the tide. Those companies are exactly what they appear to be: outliers, that is, industries or companies that for one reason or another are benefiting from factors that are, at least temporarily, stronger than the larger forces affecting our entire manufacturing base. It is not a strategy that will work for long, either for them or the country.

During the 1990's, when the U.S. economy out-performed the rest of the world, labor productivity for U.S. manufacturers improved at twice the rate as all non-farm businesses in the United States. Even during the so-called "New Economy" of the 1990's, manufacturing was on the cutting edge of innovation. Should the world's only super-power, with the best workers and the most vibrant economy in the world, have no choice but to sit passively while its manufacturing base, a crucial part of its prosperity and international influence, bleeds to death?

Decisions, policies and choices have gotten us to where we are today. And they have to get us out.

Q: Okay, that's a pretty bleak picture, what are the steps we need to take?

A: We need to stop frivolous lawsuits and reduce energy costs. We need to bring healthcare costs under control and ease the regulatory burden. But as important as these things are, if we don't seriously engage in the rules of the game internationally, in terms of access to our market and how we'll trade, it's not enough. It will only be a matter of time before we see industry after industry follow the path of those now in crisis. We cannot sustain glaring inequities in international trade. I am not an isolationist. It's a matter of un-stacking the deck.

Q: What incentive does the rest of the world have to

give up their advantage?

A: We have to recognize that the U.S. market is the prize in the game—at least for today—but it won't always be if we lose this fight. With the most consumers and the largest market and counting, we are the engine of the world and we have almost unlimited leverage, if we are willing to use it. I can tell you that when faced with potential restrictions on access to this market, foreign countries stand up and take notice. If we are willing to get serious, to let the rest of the world know we will limit access to this market, then you will see change and you'll see it fast. The breakdown in world trade talks last year was obviously unfortunate, but it's a temporary setback. The countries that blew up those talks know damn well they have more to gain in the world trading system than we do. What the temporary breakdown in talks does is give us the opportunity to craft a plan to change the base and make resolution of the issues killing our manufacturing, priority number one.

Q: What do you think our agenda should be?

A: Let's start with the treatment of taxes. There is an arcane note in provisions setting up the world trading system that I'm willing to bet very few U.S. businessmen and businesswomen know about. They should. It basically says this: that certain kinds of taxes, including the Value-Added Taxes, relied upon by many of our trading partners, could be refunded when a product is exported *without* being considered an illegal subsidy. Not *can be—IS* refunded—a million times a day.

The kind of income tax principally relied upon in the U.S., however, cannot be refunded. Stacked deck? Whose fault is it? And products sold in their markets, they're subject to their VAT tax! They don't bear any of our income taxes when they sell their products here, but we have to pay a VAT tax. This is a five-plus decade run where nations that relied upon VATs have received a straight-forward illegitimate advantage in trade. There is no legitimate economic justification for the distinction, and there never has been. It was simply a case where *we got out-foxed* and agreed to an absurd provision, a gift that we have given that keeps on giving. Keeps on hurting us in international markets.

In every trade round, elimination of this disparity is identified in our law as the principal objection of the United States and, in every negotiation, it is basically ignored. There has been a lot of hand-wringing and proposals to change our tax system to mimic those favored internationally. That's largely a pie-in-the-sky notion, given the complexity of our codes and the politics involved in making such a change. The idea should be simple. Let's just make clear that we are not going to agree to any new multi-lateral trade agreement that doesn't fix the damn problem once and for all. You can't get any simpler than that.

Here's another. A recent study shows that we are at a 22 percent cost disadvantage because of things like energy cost. So what kind of energy are we promoting? Windmills. What energy is China promoting? Huge, thousand-plus megawatt hydro-plants. There are nuclear plants in Europe and China. What are we pushing? Natural gas, because it's clean-burning.

Still, all these peaking electric plants built in the last 15 years use natural gas, but guess what the joke is? When you want the gas to run the plants, you can't have it because they won't let you drill for it anywhere. Who's kidding who? We are over-regulated with a Superfund law. And if it needs to get cleaned up, fine. But level the playing field. Over there, they get government subsidies day in and day out to clean it up. We don't. Level the playing field.

Health care costs? I'm not saying we should have a government-run health care system, but let's recognize that the rest of the world does. Let's recognize that those companies don't have to deal with the cost. There's got to be a way to unstack the deck. I'm not saying we need health care run by the government—although it could be that—I'm saying that this is a major cost disadvantage that we have: governments of the world giving their manufacturers cost advantages and we need to deal with it.

Another problem: judges give verdicts that give big dollars to trial lawyers who do what with those big dollars? Well, they give big contributions to politicians. To do what? To make laws that further burden us and drive up our costs, while appointing judges who are favorable to those kinds of rulings.

What a mess! Right or wrong, we need to recognize that the rest of the world doesn't deal with this stuff.

Q: What does the rest of the world do that we don't do?

A: China and Europe are geared up to nurture manufacturing. Why? Because they know what it brings. They know what we've already learned because we've showed them. We showed everybody how well it works. Now they want it. They can't take it by force, but they have other ways of taking it from us. Kid yourself not. Loans in China? When was the last time you got a loan from a bank that didn't care if it got repaid? Happens every day in China. There is more bad debt over there than you can shake a stick at. You don't have to worry about paying back debt, let alone the interest. What kind of advantage is that? It's all part of the nurturing process that the government provides itself because it owns 90 percent of the manufacturing. China uses a Value Added Tax because it discriminates in favor of domestic manufacturing.

Everything I've told you up to now that puts us at a disadvantage is dwarfed by the currency issue. Healthcare, taxes, energy—all those issues equal 22 percent more cost on the back of American manufacturers versus Asian or European manufacturers. China has manipulated its currency since the mid-1990s and maintains a 40 percent to 50 percent cost advantage because of currency manipulation. That's right out of the box.

Charlie Chang wants to start a steel mill over in China, and Dan DiMicco wants to start one over here. Before we do a damn thing, they have a 50 percent cost advantage just because of the currency. Remember now, in places like China, the government controls the currency policy. The government owns 80 percent of all manufacturing. China manipulates their currency. Japan floats theirs. What China does, is deliberately keep their currency weak. Billions and billions and billions of US dollars support currencies around the world every day so they have an advantage for exports.

This currency issue is the biggest issue of all and yet we can't get our administration to recognize it. We had a bi-partisan commission formed in 2000 come out with their findings to investigate, to analyze the economic and national security implications of the U.S. and China relationship. In their 2004 report to Congress, it highlighted that a U.S. trade deficit with China has contributed to the erosion of manufacturing jobs and the jobless recovery in the United States. Secondly, [it found] that manufacturing is critical to our national security. And finally, that the deficit has adversely impacted other sectors of the economy as well.

The recommendation was based on the understanding that there was no concrete progress by the administration in moving China toward a substantial upward valuation of the Yuan against the dollar and re-pegging the Yuan to trade-weighed currencies. So Congress directed the administration to take action to combat China's exchange rate practices. This currency issue is coming to a head and not just out of the mouths of manufacturers. **[Editor's Note: China devalued its Yuan in July 2005, by no longer pegging it solely to the US dollar, though its value still depends upon multiple currencies, including the US currency—a move that U.S. manufacturers and some analysts said was not going far enough.]**

We all lose our jobs when factories close. We are all workers. If Paul Revere were alive today, he'd be shouting, "The Chinese are coming!"

• •

ON THE COFFEE TABLE

Forbes, Fortune, Business Week, Steel Week

and

Steel Business Briefing

• •

We have to bring balance back to this issue. That's what's missing—balance. Do we hide behind the wall until they surround us? I say: let's understand how the Chinese government nurtures manufacturing and how the U.S. government burdens manufacturing. We have to make a fundamental choice that having a strong manufacturing base is important. And then we have to learn what we have to do to allow manufacturing to compete on a level playing field and not against a stacked deck.

In the 200 years in this country we have learned what makes a good business and what makes a bad business. We've learned what makes a good government and a bad government. We've turned our backs on the barons of big business. We've turned our backs on socialism. We've learned a lot. We shouldn't give away that experience, that knowledge and what we've built from that learning.

It makes no sense now, after all that struggle and effort, to turn around and accept a system of global trade that ignores what we have created and penalizes those that played by the rules. Our economic system is one of great accomplishment, and it's one of the greatest accomplishments of our civilization—indeed of any civilization. It would be the height of folly to do nothing while it's undermined by unjust trading rules.

After World War II, what did we do? Rather than lording our prosperity over the rest of the world, what did we do? Besides sending our men and women to die on the beaches of Normandy and elsewhere, we engaged the world to help other nations enjoy the benefits that we fought so hard to obtain. Through five decades of trade negotiations we have bent over backwards in an effort to build a global trading system that would be fair to all.

• •

HOBBIES

Ballroom dance lessons, driving vintage American cars.

—"I collect 50s and 60s models of Corvettes and Camaros. My favorite car is 1967 Corvette. All Corvettes are red."

• •

Today, however, our idealism—and that's just what it is—is being trampled upon by many other countries. We are yoked to a system that rewards not the best companies, but those with an unfair tax system, the most government subsidies, and those with the most support from their home government in currency markets. This must not continue. People have to stand up and say we're mad as hell, and we're not going to take it anymore.

Q: Isn't off-shoring the result of U.S. investors demanding a better return on their stocks?

A: The market is a wonderful thing, and you can't blame people for doing what they're doing. We're not trying to stop every off-shore job, every company from moving overseas. There are some fundamentals that are out-of-whack. We want the system to come back into balance. Then you won't find companies moving overseas because of cost. These are the jobs for our children and grandchildren, jobs for the future of our country. We have to fight for a balance. Let our workers compete and let our companies compete without an 800-pound anchor around their necks. The trading system is out-of-whack and we negotiated it away, either out of the goodness of our hearts or the fatness of some people's wallets, however you want to look at it.

Q: Aren't most manufacturing jobs union jobs? Isn't that a factor? Why do the unions support Democratic politicians?

A: First, I would say that unions in this country, whether in manufacturing or outside manufacturing, are not the force they used to be. A lot of manufacturing in this country, the jobs are non-union. Our company is non-union and 10,000-jobs strong. Sixty percent of the steel jobs are non-union. As to why unions support the Democrats, they feel let down by this administration. They don't feel like they're going to get the full support on the issues that I've been talking about. It's not all about the unions.

Labor costs are a pimple on the back of an elephant anyhow. Our total labor cost is about seven to eight percent. The freight to get it from China to here is three times that. It was two times that a year ago. The labor component is a non-issue. People try to make it an issue but it's a non-issue. It's all these other things: a 50 percent cost differential because of currency manipulation, 22 percent cost differential because of health care, tort reform and energy issues.

Q: Your company has bucked the trend. Why can't other companies generate the same results?

A: In any industry, you're going to have winners and losers, no doubt about it. If you follow the U.S. steel industry over the past 30 years and particularly over the last three years, you'll see a major change taking place in the way the industry is organized. Companies come in and buy up bankrupt companies, and bring them back more Nucor-like. They're still unionized but there are a lot of Nucor look-alikes. It has spread. The industry today is a lot healthier that it was. But even a company like Nucor is barely profitable. We made 11 cents a share being one of the lowest cost producers in the world, a year ago this quarter. We made twenty cents a share the quarter before that. You're not earning your cost of capital. You're not even coming close to earning your cost of capital.

So, yes, there are always going to be winners and losers, but we are on the same damn ship. And if that ship is sinking? You may have inefficient companies in steerage, and you may have the Nucors of the world on the top deck, but when that ship sinks, you're all drowning. And the issues I'm talking about today will impact even the best companies in the world.

We're not asking for government handouts. What we want is a damn level playing field. Only the government can do that. They've given it away and we want it back. It makes me sick to have to rely on the bureaucrats and the government and politicians to make that happen, but the reality is they're the ones who got us here, and we need them to get it back.

40

⚙Dive Deep

Michael Feiner, *Columbia University, School of Business*

Michael Feiner takes a literal approach to leadership; leaders need to write down their thoughts, worries, and fears and do it daily for insight into success and failure. They should also engage in "hand-to-hand" relations and do it hundreds of times a day.

Feiner, a former Pepsi-Cola executive and now a professor at Columbia University's Graduate School of Business, won the Surendra S. Singhvi Prize for Scholarship in the Classroom. The prize is significant, as Singhvi was considered the best teacher at the university in the eyes of a graduating class of high-achievers.

Feiner's approach to leadership revolves around a series of 50 unusual laws: *The Law of Making Your Own Bed, the Law of*

Building a Cathedral, the Law of the Onion, the Law of Tell Your Cat! and *the Law of Loyalty vs. Insubordination.*

Question: What is the essence of leadership you take, these days?

Answer: My theme is that leadership is not about great oratory or personal charisma or grand strategy or blinding technical skills. That's 10 percent of a leader's job. My mantra is that leadership is about building and managing relationships up, down, and across in an organization. It's what I call the 'hand-to-hand combat' of a leader's job. It's the up-close-and-personal interactions of a job that determine whether you're successful as a leader. Leadership is much less about pushing people, the exercise of power, and directing people, than about pulling people and taking them with you and building a "follower-ship."

You don't do that with great speeches and personal charisma. You do that with the hundreds and hundreds of transactions you have everyday.

Q: For many people, the guy at the top sits over in the corner office. Folks try not to make eye contact with him in the hallway because he's an authority figure. The only time many see him and need to think about what he's saying is when he's giving some speech, which is probably less than five percent of his time. So those speeches take on a great deal of importance to the troops, no?

A: I don't think so. I don't think so. I'm not suggesting that being good at the podium is not important. And I'm not suggesting that telling people a couple of times a year what your strategy is and what your vision is isn't important. But frankly, people today have 50 pounds of potatoes to put in a five-pound sack. No matter their level in the organization—journalist, consumer products company first-line supervisor, whether you work at Microsoft—folks are so busy that the messages from those exhortations are quickly forgotten.

People are frenzied with too much to do and too little time to do it. Effective leaders understand this and therefore, day-in and day-out—not once, or once a quarter, or whatever—

they're reminding people of their agenda and reminding people about their priorities or asking people if they are on track or are seeking feedback about whether people are on the same highway.

People get so many messages and in-boxes are so full that speeches lose much of their cachet or their power, and it happens within days, let alone weeks or months. If people are using speeches as a substitute for those hand-to-hand combat moments, the heavy lifting of day-in and day-out, one-on-one, one-on-two, or one-on-three, they're going to be dissatisfied because people are not going to be on the same highway. People are going to be complying with directives, but they won't be very committed. It's not what leadership is about. If leadership were that simple, you would get up and give a couple of great speeches and everything would be fine.

· ·
CDs in the Changer

"People are going to think I'm a bumbling old fool but I love Edith Piaf."

Dino: The Essential Dean Martin

The Long Run **by The Eagles**
· ·

But you look at great leaders over time: Churchill was a great orator, but he was also very involved in the decisions involving troop deployment. Lincoln was also very involved in picking generals and exhorting generals and challenging generals. We think of him as the Gettysburg Address, but leaders get in deep. They dive in deep. They get into the details. They tell uncomfortable truths. They build coalitions and alliances. They solicit feedback. They get to know their people. They know what makes them tick. They know how to hold them accountable. It's much more than being a great orator.

Q: It's very difficult to tell someone up the totem pole something they don't want to hear. You've got to reach up there between your shoulder blades and find a backbone and

say, "Here's the truth." Talk about the line between loyalty
and insubordination.

A: I happen to think that one of the most important
books on leadership was written in 1837 by Hans Christian
Anderson: *The Emperor's New Clothes.* No one is willing to tell
the Emperor that he's naked because the Emperor is always
right. The Emperor is supposed to know more. The Emperor is
omnipotent. I think effective leaders, high-performance leaders,
know how to tell the Emperor that the leader has no clothes.

The fact of the matter is that leaders at all levels of an
organization are in the dark. They have a very filtered view of
what's going on in the organization. So true leaders have to tell
the boss when they are naked or half-naked. And yes, you have
to do that with savvy. You have to do that with diplomacy. But
when you do it, you do it so the boss thinks you're doing it
out of loyalty to him. Not out of insubordination. Not because
you're just truculent or intransigent. You're doing that because
you care about his or her success, his or her own good, his or
her self-interest. I think organizations don't work because the
boss isn't told. The boss isn't informed. The boss isn't given
feedback about how things really are going a few levels down
in the organization.

The leaders I saw throughout my career—and my job
was to advise and counsel leaders—they understood this as
their responsibility. They were accountable for telling people
that things weren't working right. They knew how to do that.

• •

BOOKS ON THE NIGHTSTAND

Against All Enemies **by Richard Clark**

The Teammates **by David Halberstam**
—*"Even though Ted Williams was insufferable, difficult and
over-bearing, his teammates really loved him."*

• •

**Q: You're still teaching. What's on the minds of the
next generation of business leaders? What are they asking
you? What are their fears? And which are grounded, in your
estimation?**

A: The biggest fear is the knucklehead boss. Ironically, it's not any different than the questions I'm asked by middle managers and senior managers when I teach in Columbia's executive programs, right? Everybody is going to work for a knucklehead. It's not a question of *if* you're going to work for a knucklehead; it's a question of *when* and *how often.* The world is filled with knuckleheads, but who you might think is a knucklehead, I might think is a good boss. So in a very tactical sense, some of the most common questions that are asked are: What do I do when my boss doesn't know I exist? What do I do when my boss doesn't give me credit for the work I do, if he steals my ideas, if he isn't willing to give me feedback, if he treats me like a pencil sharpener?

• •

ON THE COFFEE TABLE

The New York Times Magazine

and

The New Yorker
—"I read it every week."

• •

In a higher-order, over-arching sense, I think students today—perhaps from the scandal debacles of the last few years with Enron, Anderson, HealthSouth, Worldcom, and Tyco—I think students are more concerned about what do you do when the boss asks you to do some things that are inappropriate, unjust, or unethical. I do think they're more concerned today about these things than they were six years ago.

When I started teaching during the dot-com era, it was all about money, power, fame and fortune. That was about the only thing on their minds then. So in some ways, their concerns are a good thing.

Columbia Business School is remarkably diverse and I'd say a third of my students are not American. Sometimes you have some Asian students who worry about *pushing back against the boss.* That's sort of counter-cultural in Asia. They want to know how you'd do that a little differently in Asia. But they understand that the world is different today, and organizations do work as they should. They understand that you need to be an agent of change and tell the boss above what's really going on. I don't really see much difference in this among nationalities.

And I think, as a group, they really are very concerned about ethics and values, which is a good thing.

Q: You go into a room to speak. Surely you're met with more than a little skepticism. How does one overcome that?

A: I do it by establishing my credentials. For 20 years I was a corporate consigliore and advised leaders at a variety of levels, especially the senior level in the last 10 years of my career, on what they might do to be more effective. And one of the things I think is very important to recognize is that leaders, even the most talented, even the most successful, still want to know how they should go about doing this or that. For example, how do I handle this conversation where I'm going to have to outplace Joe? How do I have this conversation with Nancy where I tell her that she's not going to get the big job of her dreams? What do you suggest we do with regard to reorganizing? How do I get the support of the corporate group to do that?

• •

FAVORITE CONDIMENT

A-1 Sauce
• •

People would ask 10 or 20 questions like that every day. It's amazing. And the notion that people put their pants on one leg at a time? It's bloody true. These were very talented, very gifted, very successful people. They knew what they were supposed to do. They knew they were supposed to motivate and inspire and align the team, enlist the support of their boss. There isn't a person in the executive suite who didn't know that. The issue is always, "How? How do you do that?

I try to say very early on that smart leaders are always looking for a point of view. They're always looking for advice. Smart leaders are always asking for input before they decide how they're going to go about doing something. I saw how difficult it was to lead. I saw what it takes to lead. I learned on real time.

Usually, within a fraction of the time I'm there, people will pay reasonably close attention and, if I'm compelling and persuasive during the talk, they walk away saying that was useful and valuable. I don't talk about theory and concepts from 35,000 feet. They don't care about that and I don't care about that. I care about the *hows* that are helpful in being more effective. People learn by stories. People remember by stories, and I use stories as a vehicle for people to learn.

Q: Keeping a journal—should executives do it? Fifteen minutes a day? A half-hour?
A: That's very helpful. I think that it's very helpful. I still look at a journal I kept when I went on an Outward Bound trip. They dropped us off on Hurricane Island in Maine and we had to keep a journal for 12 hours. I was in my early 40's, a young vice president, a big job. I still look at some of those insights. Stories are what people will remember. And it convinces people because everybody makes mistakes, including very successful executives. Everybody loves stories.

Q: You have laws of organizational behavior. What's your favorite law?
A: I love The Law of Building a Cathedral. I do think that jobs are not enough for the soul. I do think that people need meaning and purpose in their lives. And I think people need meaning and purpose whether they work in a call center, whether they work in a factory, or whether it's in an executive suite. The notion that only people who work in higher level jobs need meaning and purpose is preposterous. I love the fact that Fred Smith, chairman and chief executive of FedEx, says that they constantly remind their drivers that they're involved in the most important commerce in the history of the world; they're not delivering sand and gravel, they're delivering someone's chemotherapy treatment. They're delivering a part that may keep an F-18 flying. They're delivering a legal brief that may decide the case. I love that story because I do think that executives need to understand, leaders need to understand,

that sure, shareholder value, quarterly targets, profit goals, sure they're important, but that's not what hooks people—including executives, I might add. People need to think they're part of something that is important.

The Law of Personal Commitment for me resonates. I had relentlessly high standards as a leader. I was a tough boss in terms of what I expected out of my people, but I got it. And they cut me a lot of slack because they knew I really cared about them, and not just because their productivity would make me look good. I cared about them because I cared about *them*. I cared about their success. I cared about their career. I cared about their performance. Not just my own success and performance. When people know you care, when people know you have some share-of-mind in your solar system for them, they cut you a lot of slack and they'll kill for you.

Leadership is not charisma or oratory. Leadership takes application, stamina, hard work, perseverance, and it takes discipline.

Plus

John Eckberg

41

✸Synchronicity

Deepak Chopra

From the Chopra Center in Carlsbad, California, to his Soul of Leadership executive education seminars at the Kellogg School of Management at Northwestern University, spiritual leader and physician Deepak Chopra offers seemingly other-worldly advice and approaches to executives looking for breakthrough revenues and profits, while pursuing tranquility, health, and renewal. Recognized as a world leader in mind-body medicine, Chopra's approach blends yoga, nutrition, and meditation, to bring clarity and rejuvenation to the individual.

He teaches that everyone, be they an executive or file clerk, shares seven human needs—survival, safety, creative expression, achievement, belonging, self-esteem, and self-

245

actualization. He frequently lectures to packed auditoriums on tours that span the globe.

Question: University of Wisconsin neuroscientist Richard Davidson suggests meditation will decrease stress, anxiety and depression, boost the immune system, increase concentration and, perhaps, happiness, so why don't more people pray or meditate? And for those who do already, why don't they do it more often?

Answer: I think we get caught up with the idea that success is so important and that happiness is around the corner if we have a little more of something. That in the end, the premise becomes, that if you have enough money and enough things, you will be happy. It turns out to be a false premise because the more successful people become, the more their stresses increase. You are walking on a treadmill. You never get anywhere in terms of inner fulfillment. But the premise doesn't change, the premise is really part of our culture now. Advertising, media, the whole cultural mindset is based on this false notion that *things* bring happiness.

• •
CD IN THE CHANGER
The Beatles.
• •

Q: Does that same false premise apply to companies? Never enough profits? Never enough dividends? Never enough shares?

A: Yeah, yeah. And it's also this way in medicine. If we could just fix this one thing we could be healthy. We are such an action-oriented society. We think that the more violent our actions are, the more successful we will be. We have a war on terrorism. We have a war on drugs. We have a war on cancer. We have a war on poverty. We have a war on everything. Our bodies are, in fact, nothing more than a battleground for these war games that are being played in our minds. No wonder we are sick. As a society we do not think in terms of creative solutions.

John Eckberg

Q: Are more and more people coming to you, after your appearances, with worries about the pointless job— the common lament of the stressful life, the depressing household, or are people just paying more attention to the issue of stress?

A: It's not either. My audience is so self-selected and has followed my evolution and their own evolution. We kind of have grown up together so our deeper questions are how can we heal the environment? How can we create a new cultural mindset? How can we solve issues like social-injustice? How can we deal with the lack of economic freedom in poor countries? How can we resolve conflicts without violence?

We see in our own lives that there is such an immense improvement in evolution that we want to share it with others. My main activity right now is an organization I founded: Alliance for the New Humanity at *www.anhglobal.org*. We have a network throughout the world and are in the process of creating peace cells, linking them to each other and inviting people to be the change. If you want change in the world, you have to be part of the change. If you want peace in the world, you have to be at peace with yourself.

We do see people who come for stress management but a lot of people are beyond that, actually.

Q: How can individuals actively entice Synchronicity into their lives and into their work, and live in a prayerful state of being all day long? Meditate more often? Breath more deeply?

A: I follow certain rituals that allow me to experience my larger self, which is intimately connected with everything else. On one particular day, I will see the world as an extension of myself. If I look at a tree, I will see it as my lungs, recognize that without me breathing out, the tree wouldn't be there and without it breathing out, I wouldn't be there. We are inseparably one. The earth is my mother. The rivers and waters are my circulation. The air and atmosphere is my breath.

Another day I might just focus on relationships and see that they are the most important thing in existence, and how through the mirror of relationships we learn about ourselves and about everybody else. That requires a deep listening, a deep caring. Another day I might just watch my internal dialogue: *Am I coming from Ego? Or am I coming from Spirit?* If I am coming from Ego, then I'm always looking for approval and trying to manipulate. If I am coming from Spirit, then I feel much more relaxed. I see others as equals and I am independent of the good or bad opinion of others.

Another day I might just see that I'm not getting drawn into melodrama or hysteria. I watch my emotional turbulence, if I have any, and recognize that all my emotional turbulence comes from a deep need that we have to be offended all the time. That's where we nurse grievances. I might say, "Today, I release grievances."

● ●

BOOKS ON THE NIGHTSTAND

Fire in the Heart by Deepak Chopra

Good to Great: Why Some Companies Make the Leap... and Others Don't by James C. Collins

● ●

Q: I can just see all those executives in their tight ties and worsted wool scratching their ears and thinking, *What does any of this have to do with my top line? What does any of this have to do with the bottom line?*

A: Well, it has a lot to do with having a heart attack. It has a lot to do with getting into a messy divorce. It has a lot to do with kids getting on drugs and not coming home. It has a lot to do with quality of life. I teach leadership at the Kellogg School of Management. We get CEO's from all over the country, and political leaders from many other countries. It is one of Kellogg's most successful courses.

I tell them the following things. I say, "Listen you guys, you want to make more money? That's all you care about? Well, I'll show you how to make more money." We go into what influences the bottom line. How investor loyalty, employee loyalty, and customer loyalty are all linked and how to cultivate that loyalty. They like that. Customer satisfaction is a big issue. Well, how about investor and employee satisfaction? They are inseparably linked. "Your employees care a lot more and are a lot more important than your customers because if your employees are happy, they'll do a good job for your customers."

How do we cultivate that? It's a step-by-step process. It's not easy. I've done it at Harvard Business School as well. The times are right for a holistic approach.

Look at how a caterpillar becomes a butterfly. At a certain stage of its life, a caterpillar starts to become over-consumptive and voracious in its appetite. As a result, it starts to become grotesque, distorted, and diseased. Within the caterpillar, there are a few isolated cells scattered here and there—imaginary cells. By some mechanism as yet unknown, these imaginary cells start to connect with each other. When that connectivity reaches a critical mass, there is a mutation that gives rise to the genetic code of a butterfly. These imaginal cells start to use the voraciousness of the caterpillar itself as a nutritive soup, which helps them evolve. The rest of the caterpillar's body starts to liquefy and soon you have the emergence of the butterfly.

What a great metaphor for what is happening in our society today: war, terrorism, chaos, economic disparities, Enron, WorldCom, you name it. This is our nutritive soup. This is our opportunity if we can just reach a critical mass of conscious leaders. That is the basis of Alliance for the New Humanity, a network of connections—of conscious leaders, conscious business leaders, socially-responsible enterprises, and of people who care.

As long as we think we can abolish terrorism by killing terrorists, we will not have a solution. We think if you kill a tumor, you will not get a tumor again. Of course you will get a tumor, until you find out the cause of the tumor.

Q: I read that you've taken up golf. Why do so many stressed-out executives play such a stressful game as a strategy to reduce stress?

A: I know. And what's amazing is that in four hours, you can get to know everybody and can actually know intimate details about their life just by watching them play the game of golf. It's such a beautiful game actually. It's a perfect example of mind-body coordination and how your mind and emotions influence everything. It's also a game that teaches you meditation, mindfulness, attention, and even moments of transcendence. At the risk of sounding offensive to somebody, I'd say it's "Mystery School" for Republicans.

Q: You've probably heard the joke about the thunderstorm and the guy who runs out into the middle of the fairway in the lightning and holds a one-iron over his head and his foursome says, "No, no, why are you doing that?" The guy says, "Not even God can hit a one-iron." . . . So, *can* the Lord hit a one-iron?

A: Hah, I think the Lord can do anything. And in many ways Synchronicity is when God is doing something for you anonymously.

Q: Can I tell you about my recent moment of Synchronicity?

A: Yeah…

Q: I'm just back from an annual fishing trip with my pals—an awful trip for fishing. We weren't catching anything. So here were talking about *The Da Vinci Code* and the Almighty and the Spirit—we're all Christians—and I made this fairly blasphemous comment, I suppose. I said, "Well, the fishing was so lousy that Jesus couldn't catch a fish today."

A: Oh my…He was a fisher of men.

• •

Favorite Meal

Goa fish curry
• •

Q: So we immediately troll over to another bay and in that bay is the biggest fish I've ever seen in my life, floating belly-up, nearly dead. And in its mouth was a blue-gill, which I had been fishing for—they always ridicule me for fly-fishing for bluegills. I'd given up on bass. Anyhow, this huge bass was about to drown. We all looked at each other and knew; it was like this was the "Hand of God" fish.

A: That is the perfect example of God eavesdropping on your mind...

Q: That's what we said, that God probably got tired of Iraq and thought, "Hey, those three yokels are on their annual fishing trip again. This will be fun." The guy who pulled the fish from the water with his bare hands, he immediately won our contest. He brought the fish back to life and watched it swim away. We became fish saviors instead of fish eaters.

A: That is a beautiful story, a beautiful story. Events like that move you to a higher plane of consciousness and awareness. We come close to the mystery. We never solve it. And that's the way God wants it. But we know there is a great mystery and we find enjoyment just being aware of that great mystery.

Everybody has different questions. The basic idea behind everything we do is that we want fulfillment, we want joy, we want love, we want compassion, we want meaning, we want purpose. We have this idea that if we have enough *things*, we will have all the rest. But it doesn't work that way. Relationships are the most important things in life.

THE MUSIC

· ·

Spain: The Collection from Cafe del Mar compiled by Jose Padilla

Between Heaven and Earth by Ar Rahman

All My Favourite Things by A Man Called Adam

Vanilla Sky Soundtrack by Various Artists

Country Roads: Greatest Hits of John Denver by John Denver

The Best of the Three Tenors Jose Carrerras, Placido Domingo and Luciano Pavarotti

Romantica: The Very Best of Luciano Pavarotti by Luciano Pavarotti

La Boheme by Puccini, De Los Angeles, Bjorling and Beechum

The Beach Boys Endless Summer by the Beach Boys

California Project by Papa Doo Run Run (Brian Wilson)

Queen Greatest Hits by Queen

Sergeant Pepper by the Beatles

Grammy nominees 2001 & 2002 by Various Artists

Lover's Rock, Live in San Diego and Diamond Life by Sade

Drops of Jupiter by Train

Back on Top by Van Morrison

Keb' Mo' by Keb' Mo'

The Success Effect

   Best of Lightnin' Hopkins by Lightnin' Hopkins

   Best of Friends by John Lee Hooker

   It Has to be You by Rod Stewart

   With a Little Help from my Friends by Joe Cocker

   Time Out of Mind by Bob Dylan

   Classics, Vol. 13 by Nils Lofgren

   From Bessie to Brazil by Susannah McCorkle

   Room to Breath by Delbert McClinton

   The Soundtrack from *Mama Mia, Songs of ABBA*

   The Doo Wop Box: Vintage Rock and Roll by Various Artists

   No Fences by Garth Brooks

   Two Against Nature by Steely Dan

   Jethro Tull-Benefit by Jethro Tull

   Paranoid by Black Sabbath

   Everything Must Go by Steely Dan

   Love Story by Vivian Green

   Princess Nubiennes by Les Nubians

   Breezin' by George Benson

   Letter from Home by Pat Methany

   Paid Tha Cost to Be Da Boss by Snoop Dogg

The Very Best of the Drifters by The Drifters

Body Kiss by The Isley Brothers

The Isley Brothers Greatest Hits Vol. 1 by the Isley Brothers

Avalon by Roxy Music

The Nightfly by Donald Fagen

Ten Easy Pieces by Jimmy Webb

Sandanista by The Clash

Keep the Faith by Faith Evans

Another Place, Another Time and All Killer, No Filler: The Anthology by Jerry Lee Lewis

Soul Sauce by Cal Tjader

The Look of Love by Diana Krall

Bach - The Brandenburg Concertos by Johann Sebastian Bach, Martin Pearlman, Boston Baroque

The Best of Thelonious Monk by Thelonious Monk

Feels Like Home and *Come Away With Me* by Nora Jones

Crash by The Dave Matthews Band

P.S.: A Toad Retrospective by Toad the Wet Sprocket

The Very Best of Willie by Willie Nelson

Killin' Time by Clint Black

Philip Glass Symphony No. 3 by Modern Jazz Quartet

Shostakovich's 15th Symphony in A Major by the London Symphony Orchestra

Best of Broadway by Various Artists

The Very Best of Otis Redding by Otis Redding

Al Green's Greatest Hits by Al Green

The Very Best of Wilson Pickett by Wilson Pickett

Romances by Luis Miguel

Brand New Day and *Ten Summoner's Tales* by Sting

As Time Goes By …The Great American Songbook Vols. I, II by Rod Stewart

Motown by Michael MacDonald

College of Piping Celtic Festival by Various artists

Straight No Chaser by Indiana University A capella Men's Singing Group

Adagio for Strings by Samuel Barber

Verdi: Rigoletto (Complete Opera) by Maria Callas, Tito Gobbi and Giuseppe di Stefano

Viva Verdi by Various Artists

The Look of Love by Diana Krall

Romanza by Andrea Bocell

Lifescapes by Pachelbel

Mended by Marc Anthony

Shaman by Carlos Santana

The Very Best of Fleetwood Mac by Fleetwood Mac

Classic Yo-Yo by Yo-Yo Ma

Hotel California by the Eagles

The Long Run by The Eagles

On the Moon by Peter Cincotti

Genius Loves Company by Ray Charles

License to Chill by Jimmy Buffett

Wooden Leather by Nappy Roots

Soundtrack from Bad Boys II by Various Artists

The Pretender by Jackson Browne

Dizzy Up the Girl by the Goo Goo Dolls

(What's the Story) Morning Glory by Oasis

Greatest Hits by Sly and the Family Stone

Break the Cycle by Stained

Tumbleweed Connection by Elton John

Cieli di Toscana by Andrea Bocelli

The Essential Tony Bennett by Tony Bennett

Sinatra Reprise: The Very Good Years by Frank Sinatra

World Chants by Krishna Das

Music Detected by Deep Forest

Gladiator Soundtrack by Various Artists

Braveheart Soundtrack by Various Artists

Vineyard Church Praise Songs by Various Artists

A Day without Rain: The Best of Enya and *Paint the Sky with Stars* by Enya

Contemporary Christian Music by Various Artists

Best of the 50s, 60s, 70s by Various Artists

Voice of the Sparrow: The Very Best of Edith Piaf by Edith Piaf

Dino: The Essential Dean Martin by Dean Martin

Dream with Dean by Dean Martin

Dedicated to You by Joni James

Profile (The Best of Emmylou Harris) by Emmylou Harris

Bette Midler - Greatest Hits - Experience the Divine by Bette Midler

America IV: The Man Comes Around and *Johnny Cash Columbia Records 1958-1986* by Johnny Cash

Remembering the 50's by Various Artists

Muddy Waters, The Anthology 1947-1972 by Muddy Waters

The Library

Flight to Arras by Antoine de Saint-Exupery

Soulcatcher and Other Stories: Twelve Powerful Tales About Slavery by Charles Johnson

A Thief of Time by Tony Hillerman

Under a Wild Sky: John James Audubon and the Making of The Birds of America by William Souder

Quantum Physics by John R. Gribbon

Quantum Reality: Beyond the New Physics by Nick Herbert

The Elegant Universe: Superstrings, Hidden Dimensions and the Quest for the Ultimate Theory by Brian Greene

Webster's Unabridged

Alexander Hamilton by Ron Chernow

The Peloponnesian War by Donald Kagan

Goodnight Moon by Margaret Wise Brown

The Tiananmen Papers by Public Affairs Books

Exile by Allan Folsom

The House Sitter by Peter Lovesey

The World of the Country House in Seventeenth Century England by J. T. Cliffe

The Silk Road, Art and History by Jonathan Tucker

The Rainhill Trials: The Greatest Contest of Industrial Britain and the Birth of Commercial Rail by Christopher McGowan

Good to Great: Why Some Companies Make the Leap ... and Others Don't by James C. Collins

Hare Brain Tortoise Mind by Guy Claxon

Weird Ideas that Work by Robert I. Sutton

Cryptonomicon by Neal Stephenson

On Writing by Stephen King

Bird by Bird by Anne Lamott

A Writer's Book of Days by Judy Reeves

Going After Cacciato by Tim O'Brien

Small Wonder by Azar Nofisi

Reading Lolita in Tehran by Barbara Kingsolver

The Hemingway Book Club of Kosovo by Paula Huntley

The Lords of Discipline by Patrick Conroy

Death by Meeting by Patrick Lencioni

I Bought Andy Warhol by Richard Polsky

The Careless Society by John McKnght

No Word from Winifred by Amanda Cross

The Future of Freedom by Fareed Zakaria

The Process of Creating Life by Christopher Alexander

Flyboys by James Bradley

The Kills by Linda Fairstein

What the CEO Wants You to Know by Ram Charan

Exodus by Leon Uris

An Unfinished Life, John F. Kennedy by Robert Dallek

Power Failure - The Inside Story of the Collapse of Enron by Mimi Swartz

A Short History of Just About Everything by Bill Bryson

Folly & Glory by Larry McMurtry

Stalin: The Court of the Red Tsar by Simon Sebag Montefiore

The Nonpatriotic President: A Survey of the Clinton Years by Janet Scott Barlow

The Stone Raft by Jose Saramago

The Known World by Edward Jones

The Company of Strangers by Robert Wilson

First In, Last Out: Leadership Lessons from the New York Fire Department by John Salka and Barret Neville

Plan of Attack by Bob Woodward

Golf in the Kingdom by Michael Murphy

Personal History by Katharine Graham

My Life by Bill Clinton

The Success Effect

The Deming Management Method by Mary Walton and W. Edwards Deming

Five Equations that Changed the World - The Power and Poetry of Mathematics by Michale Guillen, Ph.D.

Zagat America's Top Golf Courses

The Worst-Case Scenario Survival Handbook for Golf by Joshua Piven, James Grace, Brenda Brown and Jim Grace

Jump-Start Your Business Brain by Doug Hall

The Five People You Meet in Heaven by Mitch Albom

Battle Ready by Tom Clancy

Crossing the Unknown Sea: The Pilgrimage Between Work and Identity by David Whyte

Listen Up, Leader by David Cottrell

The Connective Edge by Jean Lipman-Blumen

Robert Crayhon's Nutrition Made Simple: A Comprehensive Guide to the Latest Findings in Optimal Nutrition by Robert Crayhon

Fire in the Heart by Deepak Chopra

Seeking Firm Footing: American in the World in the New Century by Ambassador Richard S. Williamson (U.S. Representative to the United Nations Commission on Human Rights)

Michelangelo and the Pope's Ceiling by Ross King

Longaberger: An American Success Story by Dave Longaberger

Big Russ and Me: Father and Son - Lessons of Life by Tim Russert

The Probability of God by Steven D. Unwin

The 21 Irrefutable Laws of Leadership by John C. Maxwell and Zig Ziglar

Oscar Robertson, The Big O: My Life, My Times, My Game the Biography of Oscar Robertson

The Autobiography of Quincy Jones by Quincy Jones

The Witch Doctors: Making Sense of the Management Gurus by John Micklethwait and Adrian Wooldridge

It's Not About the Bike by Lance Armstrong

Sting: Demolition Man by Christopher Sandford

Winning: The Ultimate Business How-to Book by Jack Welch, Suzy Welch

My American Journey: An Autobiography by Colin Powell

Harry Potter and the Order of the Phoenix by J.K. Rowling

The Da Vinci Code by Dan Brown

The 72 Names of God: Technology for the Soul by Yehunda Berg and Rav Berg

I Am That: Talks with Sri Nisargadatta by Nisargadatta Maharaj

The Bible

Re-Imagine by Tom Peters

Leading the Revolution by Gary Hamel

Wild at Heart, Waking the Dead and Sacred Romance, by John Eldridge

The Success Effect

Naked Economics: Undressing the Dismal Science by Charles Wheelan

Against All Enemies by Richard Clark

The Teammates by David Halberstam

Adams and Jefferson: The Tumultuous Election (Pivotal Moments in American History) by John Ferling

Bushworld: Enter at Your Own Risk by Maureen Dowd

What Went Wrong: The Clash between Islam and Modernity in the Middle East by Bernard Lewis

Life from Death Row by Mumia Abu-Jamal

Winning with Integrity: Getting What You Want Without Selling Your Soul by Leigh Steinberg and Michael D'Orso

Success Runs in Our Race: The Complete Guide to Effective Networking in the Black Community by George C. Frazer

ACKNOWLEDGEMENTS
· ·

Thanks to the folks at Sterling & Ross: Charmaine O'Saerang, Lauren Hougen, Polina Bartashnik, Anyika Jordan, Brian Goff, Samantha Kopicko and publisher Drew Nederpelt, who can do it all; Don Banducci for your wisdom, insight, and robust curiosity; to the boundless Sarah Heath for your tireless attention to detail and optimism.

To Mike Boyer, John Byczkowski, Bill Ferguson, Meagan Booker, James McNair, James Pilcher, Jeff McKinney, Shirley Dees, Rick Green, Cliff Peale, Carolyn Pione, Mark Wert, Randy Tucker, Mark Ivancic, Brian Schwaner, Tom Callinan and all those who passed through the business desk of *The Cincinnati Enquirer* on their way to someplace else.

Notes: